ART AT AUCTION 1983–84

The Gospel Book of Henry the Lion, *The Sermon on the Mount* and *The Entry into Jerusalem*, one of
forty-one full-page miniatures, ten full-page carpet pages or interlaced initials and over
1,500 illuminated initials, from a manuscript on vellum, illuminated by the monk Herimann,
Helmarshausen Abbey, Lower Saxony, *circa* 1175–80
London £8,140,000 ($11,314,600). 6.XII.83
Now in the Herzog-August-Bibliothek, Wolfenbüttel, Lower Saxony

ART AT AUCTION
The year at Sotheby's 1983–84

SOTHEBY PUBLICATIONS

First published for Sotheby Publications by
Philip Wilson Publishers Ltd,
Russell Chambers, Covent Garden, London WC2E 8AA
and
Sotheby Publications,
Harper & Row, Publishers, Inc.,
10 East 53rd Street, New York, NY 10022

ISBN 0 85667 188 6
ISSN 0084–6783
Library of Congress Catalog Card Number 67 30652

Editor: Tim Ayers
Assistant Editor: Georgia Fogg
Assistant (New York): Elizabeth White

Printed in England by Jolly & Barber Ltd, Rugby, Warwickshire
and bound by Mackays of Chatham, Kent

Note
Prices given throughout this book include the buyer's
premium applicable in the saleroom concerned. These prices
are shown in the currency in which they were realized. The
sterling and dollar equivalent figures, shown in brackets, are
for guidance only and are based on the rounded rates of
exchange on 1 June 1984. These rates for each pound sterling
are as follows: Australian dollars, 1.54; Hong Kong dollars,
10.83; United States dollars, 1.39; French francs, 11.62; Swiss
francs, 3.13; Dutch guilders, 4.27; Italian lire, 2,340; Spanish
pesetas, 213; Irish pounds, 1.24; South African rand, 1.77.

Sotheby's galleries at Bond Street and Bloomfield Place are
indicated by the designation 'London', and those at York
Avenue by the designation 'New York'.

Endpaper
Toy manufacturer's catalogue, two volumes, 175 hand-coloured lithographed plates annotated in
pencil and ink, possibly Nuremberg, G.G. Fendler und Cp., *circa* 1877
London £20,350 ($28,287). 28.II.84
From the collection of the late Coenraad Frederick van Veen

Contents

SIR RUSSELL DRYSDALE
The out-station
Signed, inscribed on the reverse, *circa* 1964, 29½in by 49¼in (75cm by 125cm)
Sydney Aus$120,000(£77,922:$107,143). 13.X.83
From the collection of Mr and Mrs Michael Richards

Preface

A. Alfred Taubman

My earlier confidence in Sotheby's excellent prospects has been more than borne out by this year's outstanding results. The following pages record our successful year in salerooms around the world.

New York this past May was the scene for two major record-breaking sales. French furniture and decorations from Jayne Wrightsman's beautiful Palm Beach residence fetched $4.8 million (£3.5 million), while the Dreyfuss Collection of twelve Impressionist and Post-Impressionist paintings realized $12.1 million (£8.7 million), providing an auspicious start to an evening sale of property from many collections, which totalled nearly $40 million (£28.8 million). This established a new world record for any auction of fine art, surpassing even that held in New York the preceding May, which included the Havemeyer Collection.

In London, Sotheby's had the privilege of auctioning the Gospel Book of a twelfth-century German prince, Henry the Lion, described by many as the finest illuminated manuscript in private hands. Bought for a record £8.14 million ($11.3 million) by a consortium of banks on behalf of the German government, it made headlines last December as the most expensive work of art ever sold. In July, part of the collection of the scholar and connoisseur, the late Lord Clark of Saltwood, came to auction. Lord Clark's painting *Seascape: Folkestone* by J.M.W. Turner established a new auction record for any painting at £7.37 million ($10.2 million), overtaking Turner's *Juliet and her nurse*, which had been sold at Sotheby's New York in 1980.

Elsewhere around the world, Sotheby's dispersed the contents of the late Florence J. Gould's villa, near Cannes, to an enthusiastic crowd of international buyers in Monte Carlo. These and other selected works of art and paintings were sold in a week of auctions that realized a record total of FF 114.4 million (£9.8 million: $13.6 million).

My commentary on the year would be incomplete without a special tribute to Peter Wilson, Sotheby's chairman for twenty-two years, who died in Paris on 3 June. His creative contribution to the business of international fine-art auctioneering and to this great company are recognized throughout the world. My colleagues and I share a deep sense of loss at his passing.

Remaining on a personal note, I would like to thank the friends and collectors I have encountered in my travels for their compliments on Sotheby's enthusiasm in responding to clients' needs. Be assured that we will continue to provide the best service to every client in the 1984–85 season.

A Limoges enamel and copper-gilt plaque of Christ in Majesty, mounted with a jewelled filigree border as a book cover, thirteenth century, height 8¼ in (21cm)
Monte Carlo FF 2,109,000 (£181,497 : $251,371). 26.VI.84
From the collection of the late Florence J. Gould

Peter Wilson

Souren Melikian

Peter Wilson could have followed many paths. Tall, with just enough of a stoop to seem remotely approachable and cool blue eyes that missed little, he changed Sotheby's from a mildly prosperous firm into an international leader. In the process, he triggered the first major change in the art market in the last two hundred years or so.

Circumstances moulded a temperament in which every feature seemed balanced by a contradictory characteristic. To his native Yorkshire, he owed an earthy practicality suavely toned down by the literary atmosphere of his background. His mother, the daughter of Lord Ribblesdale, was the author of *The House of Memories*, and his grandfather was a trustee of the National Gallery; art at Eshton Hall was a familiar setting, not an obsession. Oxford lent the cultural polish, while a stint in journalism, with Reuters and the *Connoisseur* increased a natural inclination to get down to essentials. It also made him acutely aware of the potential of the media, a rare perception at that date.

A short spell at Sotheby's in the furniture department, where he was a director by 1938, was a parenthesis. War broke out. Service in counter-espionage with MI6 sharpened his human chess player's instinct and his reluctance to take things at face value; close collaboration with the United States made him familiar with American attitudes and interests at a time when very few Englishmen in his circle were. It was an exciting game. Many years ago, Peter Wilson told me that he toyed with the idea of staying on. He did, for six months, but was soon back at Sotheby's, this time in the painting department.

No sector could have offered a better stimulus. Cataloguing, then, was brief; attributions tended to reflect the owners' opinions. There were few monographs or modern catalogues raisonnés to lean on. Steered at first by Hans Gronau and later by his widow, Carmen, a Freiberg-trained art historian, Wilson learnt to look at paintings from a new angle, the scholar's viewpoint. On taking over the department, he pushed for greater precision.

It is possibly because attributions play such a crucial rôle in this field that he displayed an early awareness of the importance of getting major collections for sale; they lend attributions the aura of the owner's name. His familiarity with America, where great names mattered more than in Europe, may have been another reason.

Peter Wilson

Peter Wilson taking the sale of the Rosenberg Collection of Impressionist and modern paintings, 3 July 1979

Certainly, America had something to do with his determination to turn big sales into shows, preceded by carefully mounted publicity campaigns. The sale of the Jakob Goldschmidt Collection was his first *coup de maître*. In retrospect, it appears as a turning point in his career, in Sotheby's fortunes and the market at large. He was appointed chairman between the two sessions of 1956 and 1958.

As a first stage in the launching of the rocket, the sale of old master paintings was negotiated for months with Goldschmidt's son. Press coverage, masterminded by Peter Wilson before and after the auction, played a key part in its subsequent success, paving the way for a second major sale devoted to only seven Impressionist paintings. The twenty-one minute affair in October 1958 broke every record and the £220,000 for Cézanne's *Garçon au gilet rouge* may have done more for Sotheby's image than any of the individual works sold at far higher prices in later years.

The media dwelt on the sales with relish. Less was said about the methods that made them possible. First, there was the promotional machinery, combining the services of a specialized firm, Pritchard, Wood and Partners, of Sotheby's press office manned by Stanley Clark and his team, and Peter Wilson himself. Secondly, there was a complex and entirely new contract. Varying commission rates were applicable according to the level reached above the reserves. Beyond a certain point, Sotheby's was to cash in 100 percent of the proceeds. A blind gamble, critics grumbled. A gamble, undoubtedly so, but this was the beginning of a new type of competition for vendors, particularly in America, where Sotheby's scored more and more points until Parke Bernet of New York became available for sale in 1963.

The last season had not been good and there was no rush to buy. The French auctioneers got the first chance. They delegated their two leading professionals, Etienne Ader and Maurice Rheims, who made the trip to New York and decided there was nothing in it for them. Christie's was next in line and turned down the opportunity. Peter Wilson manoeuvred for almost a year within Sotheby's to carry the deal through, backed by Peregrine Pollen, his assistant in New York since 1958.

In the ten years that followed the 1964 merger, Sotheby's world sales grew from £17,018,525 to £75,119,722. The firm overtook Christie's and weathered the 1974–75 auction market dip. The figures reflected more than Sotheby's expansion: they revealed a dramatic change in society. Long confined to a closed élite of connoisseurs, buying at auction ceased to be a rarified pastime as its image became familiar worldwide, largely through Peter Wilson's exertions. In that decade, the first weekly column in the world press to handle the art market as a news item appeared in the *International Herald Tribune*, underlining the internationalization of the phenomenon.

Peter Wilson's third coup once again sprang from his personal experience and aims. He belonged to the generation of Englishmen for whom the Riviera was paradise in the sun. Accordingly, he created an outpost in what professionals considered a hopeless location, Monte Carlo. To launch the maiden sale in 1975, he used to the full the propelling fuel of two names that were well-known to the affluent *tout-Paris* and equally familiar to the international art-buying jet set. The Baron de Rothschild – Baron de Redé sale was a winner. PCW had sensed what all experienced observers had questioned, the readiness of the very rich to have a flutter with the art game in their favourite gambling setting.

Sotheby's first sale in Monte Carlo, 25–26 May 1975. Baron Alexis de Redé, Baroness Marie-Hélène de Rothschild and Peter Wilson with Prince Ranier and Princess Grace of Monaco

The ability to perceive the potential of a new situation and act against the conventional wisdom shared by Intelligence chiefs, financiers and conquerors was Peter Wilson's most remarkable feature. His natural inclination to steer people where he wanted them and to build up precarious pyramids of power, easily controlled, was a less endearing trait. He was not so much a leader adept at organizing teamwork as a grand master in the human chess game. People were deemed adequate in a given position rather than in absolute terms. He enjoyed the strategy as much as the poker game of the auction world.

When he resigned the chairmanship in 1980, he was in his sixty-seventh year, somewhat past the usual retirement age. He saw his shares then at an all time high; coincidence always served him perfectly. He was forthwith appointed Honorary Life President of the Group and, after A. Alfred Taubman's takeover, he continued in that capacity. He was indeed going over the final details of the Gould sale with Marc Blondeau, head of the Paris office, only a week before his death in June 1984, setting the scene for a last victory.

Paintings and drawings

THE MASTER OF THE LEGEND OF ST URSULA
Altarpiece with the Annunciation
Triptych on panel, 22¾in by 45¾in (57.8cm by 116.2cm)
London £198,000 ($275,220). 5.VII.84
From the collection of the Trustees of the London Oratory Charity

The triptych is complete and its frames are original. The master was a contemporary of Memling in Bruges, but he may have come from Brussels; he seems to have been at least in part responsible for the great influence of Rogier van der Weyden on the Bruges school. The figure of the Virgin in the present panel owes much to the *Annunciation* attributed to Rogier in the Louvre.

Opposite
BARTHOLOMAUS BRUYN THE ELDER
The Nativity; *The Adoration of the Magi*
Diptych on panel, each wing 19¾in by 14in (50.2cm by 35.6cm)
London £77,000 ($107,030). 5.VII.84

The *Nativity* (not illustrated) includes two female donors and bears the arms of the Counts of Manderscheid-Blankenheim, an important family from the Eifel mountains in the Rhineland. During the early years of his career in Cologne, between 1512 and 1515, Bruyn painted a series of small panels, all of the same size and each bearing a shield; few of the coats of arms are complete and this is the only picture with a donor portrait.

ANTONIO LEONELLI called ANTONIO DA CREVALCORE
St Paul; The adoration of the Virgin and Child by an angel; St Peter
Tempera on canvas, each 67in by 68⅞in (170cm by 175cm)
Monte Carlo FF 3,996,000 (£343,890: $476,281). 5.III.84
From the collection of the Comte de Tressan

The *St Paul* illustrated here was one of three canvases sold together last March, which had been at the Château d'Etrepy in the Marne since the early nineteenth century. Sotheby's identified the artist as Antonio da Crevalcore, who is known from a painting, destroyed in 1945, formerly in the Kaiser Friedrich Museum, Berlin; an oeuvre of five or six other works has been attributed to him.
Da Crevalcore appears to have come from Bologna, but was strongly influenced by the Ferrarese School, and Francesco del Cossa, in particular.

DOSSO DOSSI
St Jerome seated in a landscape
37¾in by 48in (96cm by 122cm)
Florence L180,800,000 (£77,265:$106,982). 29.IX.83

A *hare among plants* by Hans Hoffmann

Fritz Koreny

When Albrecht Dürer died on 6 April 1528, his name was famous beyond the frontiers of his native city of Nuremberg and, indeed, Germany. He was admired and honoured by contemporary princes and artists alike. Considering that he was regarded as a model to be copied and imitated during his lifetime, it is surprising that an artist of his standing and significance should have had neither pupils nor immediate successors. The generation that followed Dürer, the Little Masters of Nuremberg, were clearly influenced by his work and deeply indebted to him on many stylistic points, but they cannot, strictly speaking, be described as his successors.

It is all the more surprising, therefore, that Dürer's work should have become the object of an intense revival of interest half a century later, to such an extent that the term 'Dürer renaissance' has been coined to describe it. A general increase in collecting during the second half of the sixteenth century appears to have triggered this development. The taste of princely collectors, above all Emperor Rudolf II in Prague and Duke Maximilian of Bavaria, but also of wealthy middle-class patrons like Willibald Imhoff in Nuremberg, contributed decisively to the demand for Dürer's works. Demand came to exceed supply and, as a result, a surprisingly large number of artists began copying and imitating the master. Some of their names are recorded in documents, the best-known among them being Hans Hoffmann.

From 1557, or possibly earlier, Hans Hoffmann lived in Nuremberg. Whether he was of Netherlandish origin, as might be inferred from a decree of the Nuremberg city council in that year, or whether he had returned to the city after a stay in the Netherlands (perhaps as a journeyman) is not known. What is certain is that he had access in Nuremberg to the collection of Willibald Imhoff the Elder and that he made use of this opportunity to copy works by Dürer.

Willibald Imhoff (1519–80) was a member of one of Nuremberg's wealthiest patrician families. He was the grandson and heir of Willibald Pirckheimer, the eminent humanist and friend of Albrecht Dürer. As a result, he had inherited a number of this artist's drawings; and by skilful acquisition he added to them, forming an extensive and distinguished collection.

It seems likely, as Josef Heller reports in *Das Leben und die Werke Albrecht Dürers* (1827), that 'Der Maler Hans Hoffmann, welcher so vieles nach Dürer trefflich kopierte, war sein Umgangsfreund' ('The painter Hans Hoffmann, who made so many excellent

Fig. 1
HANS HOFFMANN
A hare among plants
On panel, 24¾in by 31in (63cm by 78.5cm)
London £407,000 ($565,730). 30.XI.83
From the collection of Mr N. Hartas

Fig. 2
ALBRECHT DURER
A young brown hare
Watercolour and bodycolour,
signed with monogram and
dated *1502*, $9\frac{7}{8}$in by $8\frac{7}{8}$in
(25.1cm by 22.6cm)
Reproduced courtesy of the
Graphische Sammlung,
Albertina, Vienna

copies from Durer, was his friend')[1] and it was perhaps this friendship that gained him access to the Imhoff Kunstkammer. At that time, the collection included Dürers of such importance that they also aroused the interest of Emperor Rudolf II. The scene was therefore set for the events of the following years and circumstances established that were to have a significant effect on the Dürer renaissance.

Imhoff died in 1580 and Heller suggests that he had paved the way for Hoffmann to enter the imperial service. The artist is soon to be found as court painter in Prague. From there, he approached Imhoff's heirs on behalf of his new master to initiate the sale of the Dürer collection; in return, the emperor offered the revenues from the Petschau estates in Bohemia. During the course of these negotiations an inventory was made, which lists the titles of many of Dürer's most famous drawings and studies from nature;[2] among them is no. 57 'Ein Hässlein'.

This entry refers to Dürer's watercolour study of a resting brown hare, dated *1502*, which was already famous at that period (Fig. 2).[3] It has been established that Hans Hoffmann copied it several times in watercolour and bodycolour, both on paper and

Fig. 3
HANS HOFFMANN
A hare among plants
Bodycolour on vellum,
signed with monogram and
dated *1582*, 24½in by 22⅞in
(62.3cm by 58cm)
Private collection,
Nuremberg

vellum. In this connection, it is interesting to find an entry in the imperial archives, dated October 1585, which refers to the servant and court painter of Emperor Rudolf II, Hans Hoffmann: 'für ainen mit ollfarb gemahlten haasen, welchen er in irer Maj. aigen camer gehorsamblichen dargeben, zweihundert Gulden rheinisch' ('for a hare, painted in oils, which he obediently handed to His Majesty in his own chamber, 200 Rhenish guilders').[4]

While Hoffmann's studies on vellum and paper are well known, until recently there was no trace of a hare painted in oils. This gap was filled when a panel painting was brought to Sotheby's last year (Fig. 1); furthermore, there are grounds for believing this to be the very picture executed for Emperor Rudolf II which is mentioned in the archives.

There can be no doubt that the work is by the hand of Hoffmann. In fact there is an abundance of evidence, mainly in the form of individual plant studies for the picture, providing us in this case with the sort of proof that is usually sought in vain when researching old masters.

More than a dozen copies and imitations of Dürer's *Hare* have been preserved, of which no fewer than six are by Hans Hoffmann. However, not one of his versions is an exact copy of the watercolour: Hoffmann either surrounds the hare with plants, insects and small creatures, as if taking it out of the original paper-white setting and placing it back in a natural environment, a combination of Dürer's *Hare* and *Great piece of turf*, as it were; or he uses Dürer's model merely as a point of departure and shows the hare from a strictly frontal viewpoint in extremely mannerist perspective.

The panel picture presented here for the first time falls into the first group. In this respect it resembles a study of a hare among flowers, in bodycolour on vellum, dated *1582* and bearing Hoffmann's monogram (Fig. 3); it was on the basis of their similarity that the painting was initially attributed to the artist. There is fairly close agreement between these two versions in many points of detail, for example, the lizard looking up at the hare, the frog, the snails creeping along the leaves and the wisps of straw, but otherwise they correspond only in the general features of the composition.

It is indeed an extraordinary coincidence that has preserved even closer comparative material, which at the same time provides an insight into Hoffmann's method of working. In particular, there are two carefully executed studies on vellum in the Germanisches Nationalmuseum, Nuremberg, one of which, bearing Hoffmann's monogram and dated *1583*, shows a clump of lady's mantle and a thistle (Fig. 4); the other shows a tree-trunk next to a thistle in full bloom (Fig. 5). Parts of both studies have been used in the picture, identical in every detail: Hoffmann combined the tree-trunk with the lady's mantle and merged the two thistles into one, also taking over small features, such as the twigs on the ground, the creeping snails and the empty snailshells.

Thus one fact fits into another in the mosaic of historical and artistic evidence: on the one hand, a payment to the court painter Hans Hoffmann in 1585 for an oil painting representing a hare, hitherto no more than an archival source; and on the other, the discovery of such a picture, together with a number of preliminary studies for it dated 1583. The dovetailing of the evidence makes it difficult to avoid the conclusion that the picture painted for Emperor Rudolf II has now been found.

Good fortune has thus brought to light the only oil painting of this genre as yet known by Hans Hoffmann. Inspired by Dürer's study, the artist does not conceal his source but elaborates upon it, no doubt in accordance with the emperor's penchant for natural science. In keeping with the taste of his time and certainly that of his imperial patron, Hoffmann's interpretation of Dürer's *Hare* is a perfect illustration of the Dürer renaissance.

NOTES
1. Vol. II, part 1, p. 72
2. J. Heller, op. cit., pp. 78–85
3. At least part of the Imhoff Collection, including the *Hare*, passed into the imperial Habsburg collections and is now in the Albertina.
4. W. Boeheim ed., 'Urkunden und Regesten aus der k.k. Hofbibliothek', in *Jahrbuch der kunsthistorischen Sammlungen des allerhöchsten Kaiserhauses 7/1888, II.Theil, Quellen zur Geschichte der kaiserlichen Haussammlungen und der Kunstbestrebungen des allerdurchlauchtigsten Erzhauses*, p. CCXX, no. 5456

Fig. 4
HANS HOFFMANN
Thistle and lady's mantle
Bodycolour on vellum,
signed with monogram and
dated *1583*,
17½in by 23⅜in
(44.4cm by 59.5cm)
Reproduced courtesy of
the Germanisches
Nationalmuseum, Nuremberg

Fig. 5
HANS HOFFMANN
Tree-trunk and thistle
Bodycolour on vellum,
18¼in by 14⅛in (46.4cm by 35.9cm)
Reproduced courtesy of the Germanisches
Nationalmuseum, Nuremberg

JAN BRUEGHEL THE ELDER
A wooded landscape with St John preaching
On copper, signed and dated *1599*, 10½in by 14½in (26.7cm by 36.9cm)
New York $319,000(£229,496). 19.I.84

Opposite
SALOMON VAN RUYSDAEL
Travellers outside an inn
On panel, signed and dated *1645*, 27¼in by 36½in (69.2cm by 92.7cm)
London £220,000($305,800). 5.VII.84

JAN BRUEGHEL THE YOUNGER
A cattle market in a village
On panel, inscribed, 22in by 33½in (55.9cm by 85.1cm)
London £126,500 ($175,835). 5.VII.84

JACOB VAN RUISDAEL
A hilly landscape with trees
Signed with monogram, *circa* 1650, 38¾in by 49½in (98.5cm by 125.7cm)
New York $517,000(£371,942). 7.VI.84

It has been suggested that the figures are by Johannes Lingelbach.

SALOMON VAN RUYSDAEL
A river landscape with riders on a ferry
On panel, signed and dated 1649, 35½in by 50½in (90.2cm by 128.3cm)
London £220,000 ($305,800). 30.XI.83
From the collection of the Trustees of the Mendel Furniture Settlement

PIETER CLAESZ.
Still life with a lobster
On panel, signed with monogram and dated *1641*, 25¼in by 34¾in (64.2cm by 88.3cm)
London £115,500 ($160,545). 30.XI.83

JAN VAN HUYSUM
Still life of fruit and flowers
Signed, 16½in by 13¼in (42cm by 33.6cm)
London £112,200($155,958). 4.IV.84
From the collection of Lt-Col. R. C. Allhusen

GIOVANNI FRANCESCO BARBIERI called GUERCINO
Ruben showing Joseph's blood-stained coat to Jacob
1655, 45¼in by 65in (115cm by 165cm)
Monte Carlo FF1,554,000 (£133,735: $185,221). 25.VI.84

The acquisition of this painting from the artist by the pharmacist Giacomo Zanoni is documented in Guercino's account books under the date 9 June 1655. It is a pendant to *Judith and Holofernes*, now in the Musée des Beaux-Arts, Brest, which had been purchased by Zanoni in 1651.

Opposite
FRANCISCO DE ZURBARAN
The entombment of St Catherine by angels on Mount Sinai
Circa 1631–40, 79½in by 49¾in (202cm by 126.4cm)
New York $308,000 (£221,583). 7.VI.84
From the collection of the Duc de Caraman

This altarpiece has recently been identified as the Zurbarán that once hung in the Capilla de Santa Catalina of the Convento de San José de la Merced Descalza, Seville. It is recorded there in the eighteenth century with a companion picture of the *Martyrdom of St Catherine*, now lost.

JOACHIM WTEWAEL
The martyrdom of St Sebastian
Signed and dated *1600*, 66⅛in by 48⅜in (168cm by 123cm)
Monte Carlo FF6,882,000 (£592,255: $820,262). 25.VI.84

GIOVANNI BATTISTA PITTONI
An allegory of winter and summer
Circa 1738, 59½in by 44in (151.2cm by 111.8cm)
London £52,800 ($73,392). 4.IV.84
From the collection of the von der Schulenburg family

POMPEO GIROLAMO BATONI
Portrait of a nobleman
Circa 1758–60, 38½in by 30¾in (97.8cm by 78.1cm)
London £121,000 ($168,190). 5.VII.84

NICOLAS DE LARGILLIERRE
Portrait of Frederick Augustus, later Elector of Saxony and King of Poland
51¼in by 38½in (130.2cm by 97.8cm)
New York $187,000 (£134,532). 19.I.84

This portrait was probably executed in 1714–15, while the sitter was in Paris with Raymond le Plat, the French architect hired by his father, Augustus the Strong, as artistic adviser to his court. The portrait of Augustus the Strong in the Nelson-Atkins Museum of Art, Kansas City, is similar in style and it has been suggested that the two works were commissioned as a pair.

PAULUS VAN VIANEN
Study of an oak tree
Pen and brown ink and grey wash over
black chalk, *circa* 1604,
5⅜in by 5⅜in (13.7cm by 13.7cm)
Amsterdam DFl25,520 (£5,977: $8,286).
15.XI.83
From the collection of Martin Reinicke

Van Vianen used this study for a silver
relief, now in the Rijksmuseum,
Amsterdam. On the reverse are studies of
ruins in brown ink over black chalk.

ROELANDT SAVERY
*A Bohemian peasant seated
on the ground*
Pen and brown ink over
black chalk, inscribed,
circa 1607–1608, 6in by 6⅞in
(15.3cm by 17.5cm)
Amsterdam DFl116,000
(£27,166: $37,662). 15.XI.83
From the collection of
Martin Reinicke

JACQUES CALLOT
An army leaving a castle
Brown wash over black chalk, $3\frac{7}{8}$in by $8\frac{1}{2}$in (10cm by 21.7cm)
London £26,400 ($36,696). 2.VII.84

HUBERT ROBERT
View of the vaulting in St Peter's, taken from an upper cornice
Red chalk, $13\frac{1}{4}$in by $17\frac{3}{4}$in (33.5cm by 45cm)
New York $33,000 (£23,741). 18.I.84

PIER FRANCESCO MOLA
Study of a boy, lying on his side
Black and red chalk, 8⅜in by 14⅜in (21.2cm by 36.6cm). New York $17,050(£12,266). 18.I.84

GIOVANNI BATTISTA TIEPOLO
View of a villa, with figures on the steps before it
Pen and brown ink and wash, 6in by 10¼in (15.3cm by 26cm). London £46,200($64,218). 2.VII.84

JACOB CATS
February: men cutting ice
Watercolour, signed, inscribed and dated *1794* on the reverse,
8⅛in by 11⅛in (20.8cm by 28.4cm)
Amsterdam DFl44,080 (£10,323: $14,312). 14.XI.83

JOHANN LUDWIG BLEULER
View of Bad Ragaz
Gouache, signed and inscribed, 12½in by 18¾in (31.8cm by 47.8cm)
Zurich SFr 20,900 (£6,677: $9,248). 26.XI.83

THOMAS GAINSBOROUGH, RA
Portrait of the Rev. John Chafy
Circa 1750, 29in by 23¾in (73.7cm by 60.4cm)
London £99,000($137,610). 5.VII.84
Now in the Tate Gallery, London

Although this portrait has long been recognized as an early Gainsborough, it was not understood why a Dorset vicar, educated at Cambridge and married to a Derbyshire heiress, should have been painted by him. However, in the course of cataloguing, it was discovered that Chafy was curate of Great Bricett in Suffolk between 1749 and 1752; Gainsborough is known to have returned to Suffolk in 1748.

HANS EWORTH
Portrait of Margaret Clifford, Lady Strange, later Countess of Derby
Inscribed and dated *AETATIS X . . ./M.D.L.X.*, 38½in by 24in (97.7cm by 61cm)
London £74,800($103,972). 5.VII.84
Now in the Tate Gallery, London

As Henry VII's great-granddaughter, Margaret Clifford considered herself heir
presumptive to Elizabeth I; according to John Camden, she was much taken
with prying into the future and 'consulting wizards'. In the event, the queen
outlived her by seven years.

GEORGE STUBBS, ARA
A bay stallion beneath a large tree; A mare and foal
Circa 1760, 45½in by 32in (115.6cm by 81.3cm) and 45½in by 30¾in (115.6cm by 78cm)
London £132,000 ($183,480); £77,000 ($107,030). 5.VII.84
From the collection of the late Pierre Jeannerat

These hitherto unrecorded paintings can be compared with the three large canvases by Stubbs, painted for Charles, 3rd Duke of Richmond, now at Goodwood House in Sussex.

Opposite
JOHN FERNELEY, SENIOR
Portrait of Frank Hall Standish Esq. on horseback
Signed, inscribed and dated *Melton Mowbray/1819*, 39in by 49in (99cm by 124.5cm)
London £50,600 ($70,334). 16.XI.84
From the collection of the late Brigadier Sir Ralph Rayner

JOHN FERNELEY, SENIOR
The Quorn – Sir Harry Goodricke's hounds at the whaw-hoop
Circa 1833, 58½in by 107¼in (148.6cm by 272.4cm)
London £57,200 ($79,508). 14.III.84

Goodricke became Master of the Quorn in 1831. He commissioned Ferneley to paint a number of sporting pictures, including this large canvas, which was still unfinished when Goodricke died suddenly in Ireland in 1833.

JOHN SINGLETON COPLEY, RA
Portrait of John, 2nd Viscount Dudley and Ward
Inscribed, 55in by 45¾in (139.7cm by 116.2cm)
London £55,000 ($76,450). 14.III.84

This painting was exhibited at the Royal Academy in 1804. It was painted while Copley was working
on *The death of the Earl of Chatham*; Chatham had collapsed and died in the House of Lords
on 7 April 1778. The unusual composition shows the sitter in profile and relates to the larger canvas,
completed in 1781, which includes fifty-five portraits of peers.

SIR JOSHUA REYNOLDS, PRA
Portrait of William Robert, 2nd Duke of Leinster
49¾in by 40in (126.4cm by 101.6cm)
London £165,000 ($229,350). 5.VII.84
From the collection of the Duke of Leinster

This painting was exhibited at the Royal Academy in 1775. Executed when the sitter was twenty-six, it shows the Duke with his hand on a document relating to the city of Dublin, where he was MP from 1767 to 1773.

ROBERT SALMON
An armed merchantman in two positions under sail off Liverpool
Signed with initials and dated *1807*, 26½in by 42¾in (67.4cm by 108.6cm)
London £61,600($85,624). 14.III.84

RICHARD PARKES BONINGTON
French coast with fishermen
1825, 17in by 21in (43.2cm by 53.4cm)
London £154,000($214,060). 14.III.84

JOSEPH MALLORD WILLIAM TURNER, RA
Neapolitan fisher-girls surprised bathing by moonlight
On panel, 25in by 31in (63.5cm by 78.7cm)
London £209,000($290,510). 16.XI.83

This painting was exhibited at the Royal Academy in 1840.

SIR EDWIN HENRY LANDSEER, RA
A highland landscape
On board, 8in by 9½in (20.3cm by 24.2cm)
London £60,500($84,095). 14.III.84

JOSEPH MALLORD WILLIAM TURNER, RA
The Splügen Pass
1842, 11½in by 17¾in (29.2cm by 45.1cm)
New York $275,000 (£197,842). 29.II.84

Turner's four visits to Switzerland resulted in twenty-six finished watercolours. The artist seems to have thought that this was the finest of them and John Ruskin considered it to be 'the best Swiss landscape yet painted by man'. Ruskin wanted to buy it in 1842, but it was not until 1878 that a group of friends acquired it for him.

Opposite
JOSEPH MALLORD WILLIAM TURNER, RA
The volume of birds painted from nature at Farnley Hall, Yorkshire
Twenty mounted studies, watercolour over pencil, thirteen signed or inscribed, bound in tooled red leather with lock, inscribed on front cover and dated *1810*, with the Fawkes coat of arms on the back cover, the volume 17¼in by 12¾in (44cm by 32.4cm)
London £220,000 ($305,800). 12.VII.84

These watercolours were probably painted in the summer of 1810 on Turner's second visit to the Yorkshire estate of Walter Fawkes, Farnley Hall, near Otley. Fawkes had been the artist's most important patron for some years; he owned over 200 Turner watercolours and drawings, as well as seven paintings, at his death in 1826. This group of bird studies was presented by Turner to his friend; they were bound in an album later. Four more watercolours of birds can be associated with the set and a number of other surviving works were executed on his visits to Yorkshire. Turner received annual Christmas boxes from Farnley of goose pie and game until his death in 1851.

THOMAS GAINSBOROUGH, RA
Mountain landscape with bridge and gorge
Black chalk and stump and white chalk on brown paper, *circa* 1786,
10⅛in by 14in (25.7cm by 35.5cm)
London £17,600 ($24,464). 12.VII.84

THOMAS GAINSBOROUGH, RA
Open landscape with herdsman and cattle
Black chalk and stump and white chalk on grey paper, mid-1770s,
9in by 12½in (22.9cm by 31.8cm)
London £35,200 ($48,928). 5.VII.84
From the collection of the late Lord Clark of Saltwood, OM, CH, KCB

JOHN CONSTABLE, RA
Worthing
Grey wash over pencil with pen and grey ink, inscribed and dated
Worthing/Wednesday 22d Sep 1824, 7in by 10⅛in (17.8cm by 25.7cm)
London £33,000 ($45,870). 15.III.84

JOHN CONSTABLE, RA
A lock near Newbury
Pencil, inscribed and dated *Lock near Newbury/June 5. 1821*,
6½in by 9⅞in (16.5cm by 25.1cm)
London £35,200 ($48,928). 15.III.84

This is one of six dated drawings that Constable completed during a stay at the
'Pelican' in Newbury, while accompanying Archdeacon Fisher on his Visitations
in Berkshire.

JOHN SCARLETT DAVIS
The library at Tottenham, the seat of B. G. Windus, Esq.
Watercolour with stopping out, heightened with gum arabic, signed and dated *1835*,
inscribed on the backboard *Library at Tottenham/of Benjamin Godfrey Windus/by
Scarlett/Mary Windus and brother Arthur*, 11½in by 22in (29.3cm by 55.9cm)
London £30,800 ($42,812). 17.XI.83

Benjamin Godfrey Windus (1790–1867) was a coachmaker who lived in Tottenham.
Between 1820 and 1834 he formed a collection of approximately fifty Turner
watercolours, many of which can be identified in this view of the library, commissioned
to record them. He was later a supporter of the Pre-Raphaelites.

DAVID COX
A view of Paris
Pencil and watercolour, inscribed with notes *tiles, old tiles, yellow, slate*, 1826,
9¼in by 14½in (23.5cm by 36.8cm)
London £44,000 ($61,160). 17.XI.83
From the collection of Dr R. Harvey-Samuel

WILLIAM ELLIS
View of Matavai Bay, in the Island Otaheite
Pen and brown ink and watercolour over pencil, signed, inscribed and
dated *1777*, 13⅞in by 20⅜in (35.3cm by 51.8cm)
London £30,800 ($42,812). 26.I.84

Ellis executed this view of Tahiti after travelling with Captain Cook's
third voyage of exploration as second mate to the ship's surgeon.

JOHN FREDERICK LEWIS, RA
Jean Caradja, Voevod of Wallachia, resting on a couch
Watercolour over pencil, heightened with bodycolour, signed, inscribed
and numbered *135*, *circa* 1838–40, 12in by 18in (30.5cm by 45.8cm)
London £19,800 ($27,522). 12.VII.84

Jean Caradja was the reigning prince of Wallachia from 1812 to 1818. He
spent the rest of his life in Italy, where Lewis painted this watercolour.

The collection of the Lord Clark of Saltwood

Part of the collection of the late Lord Clark of Saltwood, OM, CH, KCB (1903–83) was sold in London during late June and July 1984. The wit and learning of Kenneth Clark became familiar to millions around the world through the television series *Civilisation*. His impressive record of public service included such posts as Director of the National Gallery through the difficult war years (1934–45), Surveyor of the King's Pictures (1934–44) and Chairman of the Arts Council (1953–60), while his books range from important studies on Leonardo (1935 and 1939) and Piero della Francesca (1951) to more general works such as *Landscape into Art* (1949) and *The Nude* (1955).

His taste was as diverse as his knowledge and through a long life Lord Clark was an inveterate collector. The sale last summer covered illuminated manuscripts, antiquities and oriental, medieval and later works of art, as well as pictures from the old masters to the twentieth-century. There were a number of works by Henry Moore, who was a close friend for over forty years.

There was fierce competition in the saleroom, the highlight being Turner's freely composed canvas *Seascape: Folkestone* (see pp. 56–57), which broke the world record for a painting. Kenneth Clark's patronage of twentieth-century British artists is demonstrated by the works on pp. 68–69. His watercolours, drawings and medieval manuscripts are also represented elsewhere (see pp. 50, 157 and 415). In total, the sale of 200 lots made £9,082,469 ($12,624,632).

Opposite
SIR ANTHONY VAN DYCK
St Sebastian given succour by an angel
On panel, *circa* 1630–32, 16in by 13⅛in (40.6cm by 33.3cm)
London £93,500 ($129,965). 5.VII.84
From the collection of the late Lord Clark of Saltwood, OM, CH, KCB

JOSEPH MALLORD WILLIAM TURNER, RA
Seascape: Folkestone
34¾in by 46¼in (88.3cm by 117.5cm)
London £7,370,000 ($10,244,300). 5.VII.84
From the collection of the late Lord Clark of Saltwood,
OM, CH, KCB

With his *Seascape: Folkestone* Turner has once again broken all records for a painting sold at auction; his *Juliet and her nurse* established a similar record in 1980 at Sotheby Parke Bernet, New York. The pride of Turner scholars and enthusiasts in such an achievement has a precedent in Ruskin's reasons for parting with one of his precious Turner watercolours, *Lucerne*, after the death of the artist: 'I wished to get *dead* Turner, for one drawing, his own original price for the whole ten', meaning the Swiss views that Turner tried to sell through Thomas Griffith in 1842. Turner, with his sharp nose for business, would have been delighted but also amazed, *Seascape: Folkestone* being a picture that he never exhibited and one that he would have regarded as neither sufficiently finished, nor with a significant enough subject, for public consideration.

Indeed, the late unfinished oils, whether of stormy seas or of sun-drenched calm landscapes, such as *Norham Castle* in the Tate Gallery, were almost entirely neglected until the twentieth century. This picture was one of the mere handful of such works to be publicly exhibited in the 1890s. The examples in the Turner Bequest did not even begin to receive inventory numbers until 1901, the last batch not being numbered until 1944.

It was Lord Clark himself, the owner of *Seascape: Folkestone*, who discovered the last cache of neglected Turners in the vaults of the National Gallery in 1939, 'some twenty rolls of canvas, thick with dust, which I took to be old tarpaulins'. In his writings he exalted such works above all the rest of Turner's output. In fact the exhibited works, often with classical or biblical subject matter, reflected Turner's eighteenth-century upbringing in the traditions and hierarchies of the Royal Academy; Turner had a strong idea of what was suitable for public exhibition. Nevertheless, it is a picture such as *Seascape: Folkestone*, in its uninhibited expression of the elements of nature, embodied in a vortex-like composition that whips the forces of sea and sky around the frail sail and plume of smoke in the centre, that epitomizes Turner's achievement at its most revolutionary.

Martin Butlin

SIR EDWIN HENRY LANDSEER, RA
Scene in Chillingham Park: portrait of Lord Ossulton
88in by 87¾in (223.5cm by 223cm)
London £187,000 ($259,930). 22.XI.83

The dead bull is one of the herd of wild white cattle at Chillingham Park, Northumberland. Landseer had painted them before, for example, in *The bride of Lammermoor* (finished 1830); Ossulton apparently decided to have an animal killed so that the artist could make a closer study on this occasion. The plan misfired badly. The bull gored a horse and tossed a keeper, who was only saved by the prompt action of Bran, Ossulton's deerhound. It has been suggested that the figure on the left is the head keeper, with his arm around the dog. The painting seems to have been commissioned by the 5th Earl of Tankerville, Lord Ossulton's father, before 1833. It was exhibited at the Royal Academy in 1836 and praised by Queen Victoria in her journal.

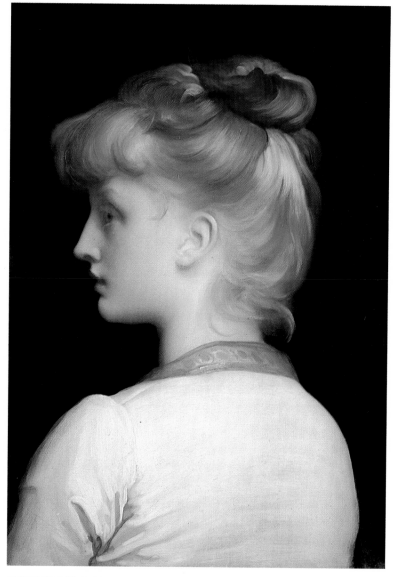

FREDERIC, LORD LEIGHTON, PRA, RWS
Profile of a fair-haired girl
Inscribed with poem on a label on the frame,
19½in by 13½in (49.5cm by 34.5cm)
London £52,800 ($73,392). 19.VI.84

The poem was written by Robert Browning, inspired by the painting:

> Yellow and pale as ripened corn
> Which Autumn's kiss frees – grain from the sheath –
> Such was her hair, while her eyes beneath,
> Showed Spring's faint violet freshly born.

The painting was exhibited with the verse at the Royal Academy in 1887 and reviewed in *The Athenaeum*: 'She is dressed in delicate milk-white, and has pale, flossy hair, her brilliant and peculiarly "modern" carnations, the extreme delicacy and softness of which characterize many of the artist's faces, are due to his training under Steinle and his studies in early Italian art.'

HARRY BRIGHT
The battle of the frogs and the mice
Watercolour heightened with white and gum arabic, signed and dated *1871*,
21 in by 34¾ in (53.5cm by 88.3cm)
London £25,300 ($35,167). 1.III.84

This painting was inspired by a mock-heroic Greek poem, 'The Battle of the Frogs and the Mice', which was at that time erroneously attributed to Homer. It was exhibited at the Royal Academy in 1871 with the quotation:

There by the banks and in armour bright
Sustain the first impetuous shocks of fight

The picture might also be interpreted as a satire on the Franco–Prussian war.

Opposite
RICHARD DADD
Bacchanalian scene
On panel, inscribed and dated *1862* on the reverse, 14 in by 9½ in (35.6cm by 24.1cm)
London £88,000 ($122,320). 22.XI.83
From the collection of the Lady Mairi Bury

The inscription reads: *Est suum cuique dunc dictum/Transupra et ecce sinistrum/Simile similibus addendum/Daemoni date debendummmmm . . .*, 'Each man then has his own unlucky fate both here and beyond – like must be added to like and one's due paid to the appointed spirit.' The picture was painted during Dadd's confinement in Bethlem mental hospital and was formerly known as *Circe*.

SIR JOHN EVERETT MILLAIS, Bt, PRA
Mrs James Wyatt and her daughter
On panel, signed with monogram, *circa* 1850, 14in by 17¾in (35.6cm by 45.1cm)
Sold by private treaty to the Tate Gallery, London

James Wyatt was a collector and art dealer in Oxford, who also acted as the curator of the Duke of Marlborough's collection at Blenheim. He owned a number of works by Millais, from whom he commissioned a pair of portraits, one of himself with his grand-daughter, Mary, and the other (shown here) of Sarah, Mary's sister, with their mother, Eliza.

In some respects, the painting can be read as a Pre-Raphaelite manifesto. The prints in the background are after Leonardo's *Last Supper*, Raphael's *Madonna della sedia* and the same artist's *Alba Madonna*. Millais held Raphael in contempt at this time; Raphael's idealized figures and flowing, harmonious compositions are used to set off the realism and awkwardness of the modern mother and child group. The artist spells out the Raphaelite nature of recent British art and offers his own style as a corrective.

SIR JOHN EVERETT MILLAIS, Bt, PRA
Nina, daughter of Frederic Lehmann, Esq.
Signed with monogram and dated *1869*, 51¾in by 34½in (131.5cm by 87.5cm)
London £253,000 ($351,670). 19.VI.84

This painting was exhibited at the Royal Academy in 1869 and reviewed by
The Athenaeum: 'Beyond question the most splendid artistic triumph in this
gathering is due to Mr Millais on account of his marvellous portrait of a very
young lady, Miss Nina Lehmann . . . which is such, with extreme freedom of
painting and surprising mastery, as none but an artist trained, as Mr Millais
was, in the manner of Titian, could happily venture on.'

SIR JOHN LAVERY, RA
The tennis party
On board, signed, inscribed *sketch for large picture* and dated *1885*, 9½in by 23in (24cm by 58.5cm)
London £31,900 ($44,341). 22.XI.83

This is a sketch for *The tennis party*, exhibited at the Royal Academy in 1886, which is now in
Aberdeen Art Gallery. Of the finished work, Lavery wrote in his autobiography (1940): 'It is generally
considered – and I think fairly – that this picture expresses my debt to French teaching. Although I
had only seen Bastien-Lepage on one occasion, . . . I had never forgotten his advice on figures in motion
. . . From that day on I became obsessed by figures in movement, which resulted finally in *The tennis
party* and drew attention to what became known as "The Glasgow School".'

JOHN DUNCAN FERGUSSON
In the park
On panel, *circa* 1905–1906, 6½in by 6½in (16.5cm by 16.5cm)
Gleneagles £8,250 ($11,468). 30.VIII.83

This picture was painted while the artist was working in Paris.

Opposite
FRANK CADOGAN COWPER, RA
Venetian ladies listening to 'the serenade' on the Grand Canal
Signed and dated *1909*, and titled on a label on the reverse, 38in by 53in (96.5cm by 134.5cm)
London £92,400 ($128,436). 19.VI.84

This painting was exhibited at the Royal Academy in 1909.

WILLIAM ROBERTS, RA
He knew Degas
Signed, 1938, 36in by 36in (91.4cm by 91.4cm)
London £36,300 ($50,457). 23.V.84
From the collection of Ernest Cooper

The painting depicts Sickert and his third wife, Thérèse Lessore, at Bathampton, Wiltshire.

Opposite
SIR GEORGE CLAUSEN, RA
The shepherd boy
Signed and dated *1883*, and signed, titled and dated on the reverse, 38½in by 26½in (97.8cm by 67.3cm)
London £57,200 ($79,508). 23.V.84

This is a previously unrecorded work.

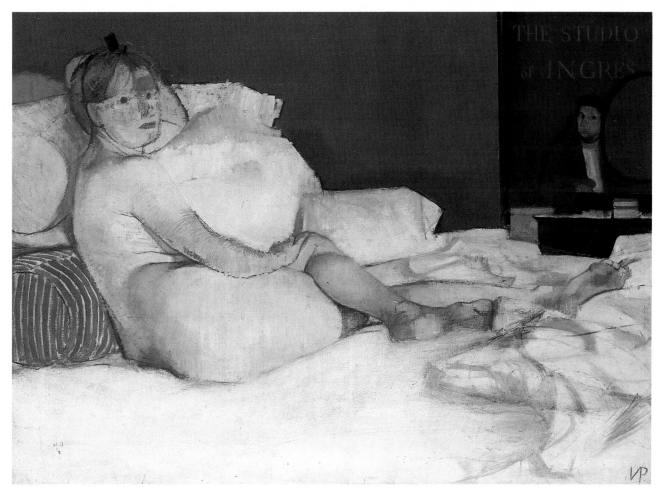

VICTOR PASMORE, CH
The studio of Ingres
Signed with initials and titled, 1945–47, 29¼in by 39¼in (74.3cm by 99.7cm)
London £59,400 ($82,566). 27.VI.84
From the collection of the late Lord Clark of Saltwood, OM, CH, KCB

As a result of Kenneth Clark's patronage, Victor Pasmore was able to give up his full-time work at the London County Council and devote himself entirely to painting in 1938. In his autobiography, *Another Part of the Wood* (1974), Lord Clark wrote of the artist: 'He was not only the most gifted painter of the group (the Euston Road School), but, in my opinion, one of the two or three most talented English painters of this century.'

Opposite
VANESSA BELL
Self portrait
1958, 19in by 15½in (48.3cm by 39.4cm)
London £31,900 ($44,341). 27.VI.84
From the collection of the late Lord Clark of Saltwood, OM, CH, KCB

The artist was nearly eighty when she painted this, her last self portrait.

JOHN SINGER SARGENT, RA
Palazzo Cavalli, Venice
Watercolour and pencil, heightened with bodycolour, signed and
inscribed, 14in by 20in (35.6cm by 50.8cm)
London £93,500 ($129,965). 2.XI.83

KARL FRIEDRICH SCHINKEL
Italienischen Märchen
Gouache and pen and ink, signed and dated *1815*,
7in by 4¾in (17.5cm by 12cm)
London £20,900 ($29,051). 21.VI.84

Opposite
DAME LAURA KNIGHT, DBE, RA
Penzance fair
Signed and dated *1916*, 46in by 59½in (116.8cm by 151.2cm)
London £26,400 ($36,696). 23.V.84

The figure in red in the foreground is the artist.

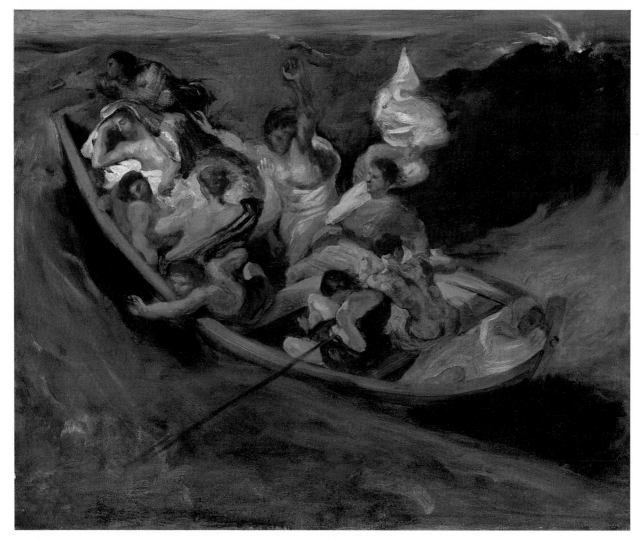

EUGENE DELACROIX
Christ on the Lake of Gennesaret
17½in by 21in (44.5cm by 53.5cm)
London £104,500($145,255). 22.XI.83

The picture is almost certainly the earliest of Delacroix's ten recorded oils on this subject, which are generally thought to have been painted *circa* 1853–54.

Opposite
PIERRE-PAUL PRUD'HON
Justice and Divine Vengeance pursuing Crime
12⅝in by 15¾in (32cm by 40cm)
Monte Carlo FF1,498,500(£128,959:$178,605). 5.III.84

This is an oil sketch for the painting commissioned by Comte Nicolas Frochot, Préfet of the Seine, for the courtroom of the Palais de Justice in Paris. The finished work was exhibited at the Salons of 1808 and 1814 and is now in the Musée du Louvre. Prud'hon gave this sketch to Frochot.

JEAN-BAPTISTE-CAMILLE COROT
Horses watering by a willow grove
Signed, *circa* 1860–65, 17in by 29¾in (43cm by 75.5cm)
New York $176,000 (£126,619). 26.X.83

ALBERT ANKER
Girl with a toy lamb (Portrait of Emilie Weiss)
Signed, 1868, 16⅞in by 20½in (43cm by 52cm)
Zurich SFr137,500(£43,930:$60,841). 21.VI.84

Opposite
WILLIAM-ADOLPHE BOUGUEREAU
Maternal admiration
Signed and dated *1869*, 51⅛in by 39¼in (130cm by 99.5cm)
New York $110,000(£79,137). 29.II.84
From the collection of the late Josephine F. Schmidt

LUDWIG DEUTSCH
The snake charmers
On panel, signed and dated *Paris 1888*, 27½in by 36¼in (70cm by 92cm)
London £187,000 ($259,930). 19.VI.84

JOSE VILLEGAS Y CORDERO
The siesta
Signed and dated *1874*, 44in by 27½in (112cm by 70cm)
New York $96,250 (£69,245). 24.V.84

MADELEINE LEMAIRE
An elegant tea party in the artist's studio
Signed, 45¼in by 55in (115cm by 139.5cm)
London £70,400 ($97,856). 19.VI.84

The musical receptions held by Madeleine Lemaire in her studio
were among the most fashionable in Paris at the turn of the
century; it was at one of these meetings that Marcel Proust met
Robert de Montesquiou, a fashionable figure upon whom Proust
based the character of the Baron de Charlus in *A la recherche du
temps perdu*. The woman seated on the right end of the sofa is
probably the artist herself.

Madeleine Lemaire at work

ALFRED DE DREUX
Portrait of Hollingsworth Magniac on his horse Eureka
29½in by 37¾in (75cm by 96cm)
London £96,800 ($134,552). 19.VI.84

Hollingsworth Magniac (1786–1867) was a senior partner in his brother's firm, Magniac,
Matheson & Co., later Jardine Matheson & Co. of Hong Kong. He assembled an impressive art
collection at Colworth House in Bedfordshire, which realized £100,000 when it was sold in July 1892.
As a keen huntsman and Master of the Oakley Hunt from 1841–47, he was a patron of the sporting
artists John Ferneley and James Aitken.

LOUIS-EMILE ADAN
Gulliver in the land of the giants
Signed, 45in by 83½in (114.5cm by 212cm)
New York $71,500 (£51,439). 24.V.84

The subject is taken from part 2, chapter 5 of *Gulliver's Travels* by Jonathan Swift (1726), where the hero is at the court of the giant Brobdingnags. As an amusement, a sailing boat was fashioned to Gulliver's specifications: 'here I often used to row for my own diversion, as well as that of the queen and her ladies . . . Sometimes I would put up my sail . . . while the ladies gave me a gale with their fans'.

JOAQUIN SOROLLA Y BASTIDA
Valencian scene
Signed and dated *1893*, 48in by 74¾in (122cm by 190cm)
Madrid Ptas 22,000,000 (£103,286: $143,791). 9.II.84

JEAN DELVILLE
Medusa
Pen and ink, blue crayon, pastel, watercolour and gold paint, signed and dated *1893*,
5¾in by 14in (14.5cm by 35.5cm)
London £20,900 ($29,051). 22.XI.83

IGNACIO ZULOAGA Y ZABALETA
A view of Toledo
Signed, 1911, 60¼in by 70¼in (153cm by 178cm)
London £57,200($79,508). 19.VI.84

Opposite
LEON BAKST
The cards
Gouache over pencil, signed, 1903, 18½in by 24¼in (47cm by 61.5cm)
London £13,200($18,348). 15.II.84
From the collection of Madame Madeleine Bakst

In 1904, Bakst published twelve of his designs for the ballet *La Fée des Poupées*, as cards to be sold for the benefit of the Red Cross. This is believed to be a design for the poster that was produced to advertise the publication. The woman is probably Liubov' Pavlovna Gritsenko, whom Bakst met around this time and subsequently married. The girl may be a daughter of Gritsenko's by a previous marriage or a niece of the artist. They are clearly looking at a set of the cards.

CLAUDE MONET
Cathédrale de Rouen: le portail (soleil)
Signed and dated *94*, 39⅜in by 25⅝in (100cm by 65.1cm)
New York $2,530,000 (£1,820,144). 15.V.84

PIERRE-AUGUSTE RENOIR
Young woman with a Japanese parasol
Signed, *circa* 1876, 19¾in by 24in (50.2cm by 61cm)
New York $2,090,000(£1,503,597). 15.V.84

CLAUDE MONET
The port at Zaandam
Signed, 1871, 18½in by 29⅛in (47cm by 74cm)
New York $962,500 (£692,446). 16.XI.83

Opposite
EDGAR DEGAS
The bath
Pastel and charcoal on paper, stamped with signature, *circa* 1888, 35½in by 28⅜in (90.2cm by 72cm)
New York $1,100,000 (£791,367). 15.V.84

The collection of Erna Wolf Dreyfuss and Julius Wolf

VINCENT VAN GOGH
La Robine du Roi
1888, 29in by 24in (73.7cm by 61cm)
New York $1,760,000 (£1,266,187).
15.V.84
From the collection of the late
Erna Wolf Dreyfuss and Julius Wolf

The centrepiece of Sotheby's record-breaking evening sale in New York on 15 May 1984 was a group of twelve pictures from the collection of Erna Wolf Dreyfuss, who died last year. Important works by Gauguin, Degas, Monet and Van Gogh were among the paintings, which had not been seen in public for more than thirty years.

Erna and Julius Wolf were married in 1923 and lived in Zurich until the outbreak of the Second World War, when they moved to New York. This group of paintings was assembled after their marriage through a lifelong friend, Morris Gutmann; Gutmann was a highly respected dealer in Impressionist and Post-Impressionist art, in Germany, Paris and then New York, where he started the French Art Galleries. Julius Wolf died in 1944, but Gutmann continued to advise Erna on acquisitions after her marriage to Sylvain Dreyfuss, in 1948.

Like the Havemeyer paintings last year, the quality of the pictures and their prolonged absence from view made them highly desirable. Gauguin's *Mata mua* fetched the highest price (see opposite). Executed during the artist's first visit to Tahiti, it is one of the few important paintings by him still in private hands. Degas's pastel *Au Musée du Louvre* is discussed here by Professor Theodore Reff (see p. 90). Van Gogh's *La Robine du Roi* depicts women washing by a canal at Arles (see above).

In total the collection made $12,171,500 (£8,756,475).

PAUL GAUGUIN
Mata mua
Signed, titled and dated *92*, 34¾in by 25¾in (88.3cm by 65.4cm)
New York $3,850,000(£2,769,784). 15.V.84
From the collection of the late Erna Wolf Dreyfuss and Julius Wolf

Au Musée du Louvre by Edgar Degas

Theodore Reff

Au Musée du Louvre (Fig. 1) is one of the most charming and sophisticated of the many portraits that Degas painted in 1879, among them such well-known works in public collections as the *Diego Martelli* in Edinburgh, the *Edmond Duranty* in Glasgow, the *Miss La La* in London and the *Mme Dietz-Monin* in Chicago. Unlike these, the double portrait of Mary and Lydia Cassatt in the Grande Galerie of the Louvre has remained hidden in private collections from the beginning, rarely exhibited and virtually inaccessible, although it has often been reproduced. The picture passed from Degas's studio through the collections of his niece Jeanne Fèvre in Monte Carlo, the connoisseur Maurice Exsteens in Paris and the reclusive Erna Wolf Dreyfuss in New York. It only emerged from this obscurity with the sale at Sotheby's. Seeing it at last, one could appreciate how well it belongs to the group of brilliantly inventive portraits painted in 1879, perhaps the highest point in Degas's long and varied career.

This was also the moment of his closest rapport and collaboration with Mary Cassatt, whom he had met two years earlier. She was by now a good friend, as well as a colleague much influenced by him in her scenes of modern urban life. Indeed, she had recently begun to exhibit with him in the Impressionist group shows and to plan with him, together with Pissarro, Bracquemond and others, a publication of modern prints to be called *Le jour et la nuit*. The antithesis evident in that title evokes, as Nancy Mathews has noted, not only 'day and night', but also those more figurative juxtapositions that fascinated both artists: 'black and white, light and shadow, young and old, ancient and modern, public and private, beautiful and ugly.' It is on just such a principle of contrast that the image of Mary and Lydia Cassatt at the Louvre is also built.

Just as Mary's slender, erect figure, debonair in silhouette and seeming to pivot on her tightly furled umbrella, conveys an energetic and independent personality, so Lydia's more compact, seated figure, demurely dressed and primly holding a guidebook before her face, projects her conventional and retiring character. Even the pictures behind them are cleverly arranged to reinforce the contrast: Mary's head appears framed by a small, brightly coloured work, whereas Lydia's more rotund figure is anchored by the larger, more sombre picture above. Yet the two women are linked by the strongly defined form of Mary's umbrella, which continues the diagonal of her outstretched arm and appears to touch the hem of Lydia's dress. Most striking of all, perhaps, as a linking device is the series of diagonal lines formed by the parquet floor

Fig. 1
EDGAR DEGAS
Au Musée du Louvre (*Miss Cassatt*)
Pastel, stamped with signature, 1879, 28in by 21¼in (71cm by 54cm)
New York $2,530,000(£1,820,144). 15.V.84
From the collection of the late Erna Wolf Dreyfuss and Julius Wolf

Fig. 2
EDGAR DEGAS
Miss Cassatt au Louvre
Charcoal and pastel, signed and inscribed, 1879,
23⅝in by 18½in (60cm by 47cm)
Photograph reproduced courtesy of Columbia
University, New York

and long bench of the gallery, lines that fly like arrows from right to left, as if to make visible one woman's gaze at the other. Through such means Degas makes every element in his brilliant design enhance the meaning of the moment that he has imagined for his unconventional portrait.

However convincing the final work may seem as an image of something observed in a Louvre gallery, it is in fact the product of many studies carefully distilled and combined, very few of which were actually made there. Like most of Degas's compositions, it illustrates his cynical yet accurate remark, 'Art is a lie to which one gives the accent of truth.' Beginning with rapid notebook sketches of Mary Cassatt in silhouette alone and a more detailed notebook sketch of her head outlined against a picture in a carved frame, which is perhaps the only study definitely done at the Louvre, he made a larger charcoal and pastel drawing of her figure down to the knees (Fig. 2), emphasizing the play of light over her close-fitting jacket and skirt. There is also a charming study of Lydia alone (Fig. 3), wearing a long, buttoned dress and high shoes, though not the hat and gloves seen in the final work, and holding the tiny guidebook before her downcast eyes; the very image of propriety. Degas then placed the two figures on a single sheet (Fig. 4), again stressing their silhouettes but entirely ignoring the background, and this he squared for enlargement in the final work.

Fig. 3
EDGAR DEGAS
Etude pour Au Musée du Louvre
Charcoal and pastel, stamped with signature, 1879,
19in by 12¼in (48.3cm by 31.1cm)
Photograph reproduced courtesy of Durand Ruel, Paris

Fig. 4
EDGAR DEGAS
Etude pour Au Musée du Louvre
Pencil, stamped with signature, 1879,
11¾in by 9½in (29.9cm by 24.2cm)
Photograph reproduced courtesy of Durand
Ruel, Paris

Fig. 5
EDGAR DEGAS
Au Louvre: la peinture
Etching, aquatint, drypoint and *crayon électrique*, 1879,
10½in by 9in (26.7cm by 22.9cm)
Reproduced courtesy of the Art Institute of Chicago
(Gift of Walter S. Brewster)

Two further drawings, showing the same figures reversed or in a different relation to each other, were evidently made in preparation for the prints that Degas worked on at the same time as the pastel.

Probably intended for publication in *Le jour et la nuit*, to mark his public debut as a graphic artist, these prints are among the most carefully developed of any in his oeuvre; the one set in the Grande Galerie (Fig. 5) went through as many as twenty states. The two figures are here in their familiar poses, clearly derived by tracing one of the drawings, but Lydia's position is reversed and the two overlap, indeed are compressed into a tall, narrow space that is made to seem all the more narrow by the marble pillar running the entire length of the left side. The space is reminiscent of that in Japanese 'pillar prints' and was perhaps influenced by them. Fascinated by the eccentric format of this print, Degas reworked an impression of it so thoroughly in pastel that its graphic origin was long unnoticed. The other print, likewise fully developed by etching, aquatint and other means (Fig. 6), shows both figures reversed but spaced as they are in the large pastel. Here the setting is the Salle du Tombeau Lydien, a gallery of antiquities dominated by an Etruscan sarcophagus from Cervetri, of which Degas made a separate drawing in order to study the complex play of light and reflection on its glass case. Lydia seems to stare beyond Mary at the object of the latter's own gaze, the figures of the husband and wife on the sarcophagus. Degas has

Fig. 6
EDGAR DEGAS
Au Louvre: Musée des Antiques
Etching, aquatint and *crayon électrique*,
1879, 11⅞in by 5in (29.9cm by 12.7cm)
Reproduced courtesy of the
Metropolitan Museum of Art,
New York (Rogers Fund, 1919)

cleverly shown them from such an angle that they in turn seem to stare at Lydia. 'In effect, then,' as I have said elsewhere, 'his image is a witty, modern equivalent of the older one, especially popular in late medieval and Renaissance art, of The Three Living Meeting the Three Dead.'

Of the dozen or so images of the two sisters at the Louvre that Degas made in a variety of media – pencil, charcoal, pastel and pastel over etching, as well as etching, aquatint, drypoint and *crayon électrique* – the large pastel formerly in the Dreyfuss Collection is undoubtedly the most important and most fully realized. The design is as complex as that of the prints, but the format is much larger and the colour adds a measure of richness and subtlety, a richness of chromatic substance at once atmospheric and tangible. The vibration of the green and blue pictures on the wall against the glowing pink of the wall itself, the resonance of Mary's reddish-brown costume and the bluish-grey of Lydia's against the shimmering beige, tan, pink and white of the floor and bench – these effects are seen only in the pastel. Yet Degas, forever dissatisfied with his work, was evidently planning to revise it further when he put it aside for what turned out to be the last time; witness the discrepancies in the colouring of the bench and wall on both sides of Lydia, and the odd, unidentifiable shape overlapping the picture above her head. This is surely why he kept the pastel hidden in his studio, unsigned and unexhibited, until his death.

CAMILLE PISSARRO
The lock at Pontoise
Signed, *circa* 1869–70, 23in by 28¼in (58.5cm by 71.8cm)
New York $632,500(£455,036). 15.V.84

Opposite
PAUL GAUGUIN
Still life with mangos
Signed, *circa* 1896, 11⅞in by 18⅝in (30.2cm by 47.4cm)
New York $1,210,000(£870,504). 15.V.84

VINCENT VAN GOGH
The steps at Auvers
On board, 1890, 8¼in by 10⅛in (21cm by 25.7cm)
London £473,000 ($657,470). 26.VI.84

AMEDEO MODIGLIANI
Seated girl in a petticoat
Signed, 1918, 31⅞in by 21¾in (81cm by 55.3cm)
New York $1,100,000 (£791,367). 15.V.84
From the collection of the Marion O. Hoffman Trust

PABLO PICASSO
Head of a woman (*Woman in pink*)
Gouache on paper laid down on board, signed, 1906, 25in by 19in (63.5cm by 48.3cm)
London £660,000 ($917,400). 26.VI.84
From the collection of Baron H. H. Thyssen-Bornemisza

HENRY MOORE
Reclining figure
Bronze, signed, numbered *4/6* and stamped with the foundry mark *H. Noack Berlin*, 1967–70,
length 135in (343cm)
New York $660,000 (£474,820). 15.V.84

ARISTIDE MAILLOL
La rivière
Lead, signed, inscribed *épreuve d'artiste* and stamped with the foundry mark *Georges Rudier Fondeur Paris*, 1939–43, length 89in (226cm)
New York $1,100,000 (£791,367). 15.V.84

EGON SCHIELE
Self portrait
Watercolour over pencil, signed and dated *1911*, and stamped with the *Nachlass* mark
on the reverse, 19½in by 12½in (49.5cm by 31.8cm)
London £121,000 ($168,190). 28.III.84

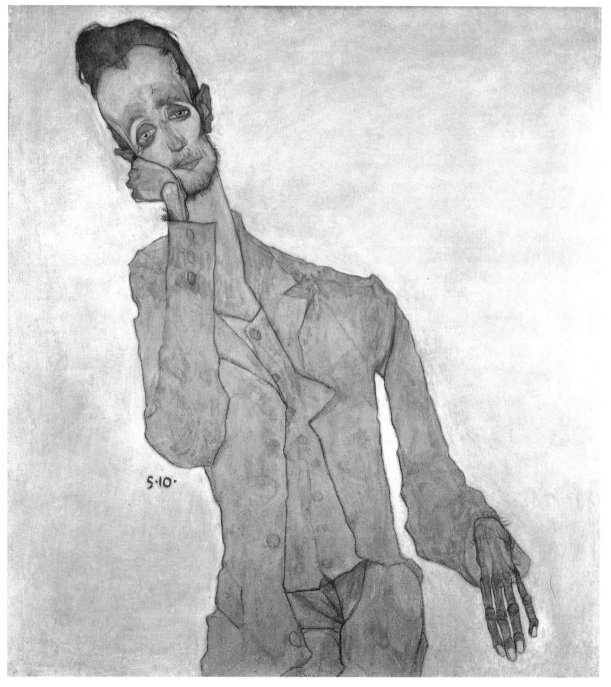

EGON SCHIELE
Portrait of the painter Karl Zakovsek
Oil, tempera and charcoal on canvas, signed with initial and dated *10*,
$39\frac{3}{8}$in by $35\frac{1}{2}$in (100cm by 90.2cm)
New York $2,420,000 (£1,741,007). 16.XI.83
From the collection of Dr Albert W. Grokoest

Zakovsek was a student with Schiele at the Akademie der Bildenden Künste in Vienna.
The composition owes much to Van Gogh's *Portrait of Dr Gachet*, which Schiele knew
from Meier-Graefe's monograph on the artist (1910).

Der Goldene Ritter by Gustav Klimt

Alice Strobl

Der Goldene Ritter first appeared in November 1903, as part of an exhibition of Klimt's collected works within the context of the eighteenth exhibition of the Vienna Secession (Fig. 1). Klimt seems to have painted it specifically for the occasion. Exhibitions were a particular spur for the artist to finish and display as many new or hitherto-unknown pictures as possible. He concentrated his energies remarkably for this event, which offered a unique opportunity to exhibit his works together and establish his reputation. Never again in his lifetime was there to be such a comprehensive show: no fewer than forty-seven paintings were included, among them the three *Fakultätsbilder* for Vienna University and the *Beethovenfries*, as well as a series of drawings.

Karl W. Wittgenstein, the father of the philosopher, probably bought the picture at the Vienna exhibition. It was in Wittgenstein's possession when Klimt wrote asking for it to be loaned to the second exhibition of the German Künstlerbund in Berlin, in 1905. The painting had also been shown in Dresden in 1904 and it was to find its way into three exhibitions after Klimt's death; once into an exhibition of Austrian art in the Netherlands, in 1927–28, and then into the Klimt memorial shows of 1928 and 1943, in Vienna. After that, it disappeared. The contemporary press gave it little coverage, but modern research has established that the figure is a variant of the knight in the *Beethovenfries* (Fig. 2). The work finally reappeared for auction last year.

The *Goldene Ritter* stands at the beginning of Klimt's mature period. The closed visor of the knight in golden armour, riding a stepping horse, suggests that he is ready for battle. Thus the picture recalls the representations of combat that Klimt had executed, particularly in his graphic work, after the foundation of the Secession in 1897: Hercules's battle against Cerberus in the background of *Tragödie*, an illustration for *Allegorien. Neue Folge*, no. 66, 1897; Theseus's struggle with the Minotaur before Pallas Athena, patroness of the arts, in the first poster of the new association of artists in 1898; and the painting of Pallas Athena from the same year, in which Hercules wrestles with a Triton. All these images focus on the struggle of creativity with the forces of reaction, in this case particularly the conflict of the Secession with the Künstlerhaus, which represented the art of the establishment.

Klimt chose as his models figures from Greek vase painting. For the *Beethovenfries* of 1903, he also drew upon Greek mythology; implicit in the subject of the *Wohlgerüstete Starke*, or 'well-armed hero', is Zeus, conqueror of Typhon and his daughters the

Fig. 1
GUSTAV KLIMT
Der Goldene Ritter (*Das Leben ist ein Kampf*)
1903, 39⅜in by 39⅜in (100cm by 100cm)
London £682,000 ($947,980). 6.XII.83

Fig. 2
Detail of the *Wohlgerüstete Starke* from the
first panel of Klimt's *Beethovenfries*, tempera
on plaster, 1902,
6ft 6¾in by 68ft (2.2m by 25m)
Reproduced courtesy of the Österreichische
Galerie im Belvedere, Vienna

Gorgons. In this case, however, the hero wears a fifteenth-century suit of armour (Fig. 2),
indicating a revival of the Romantic vision of the Middle Ages, which ties in closely
with the *Goldene Ritter* exhibited the same year.

In the *Goldene Ritter* Klimt was grappling with both the form and the meaning of
Dürer's engraving *Knight, Death and the Devil* of 1513 (Fig. 3). Klimt chose to represent
the knight alone, while hinting at death and the devil with the snake, almost exactly
where Dürer had depicted a death's head on a tree-stump. Klimt took over the tree-
stump, in three places, as a symbol of transience, and juxtaposed it to the shrub
blossoming in the background. At roughly the same time, the artist was executing
several woodland scenes, *Pinewood I* and *II*, *Beechwood I* and *II*, and *Birchwood*, in
which he was interested by the upward-growing trunks, cut off at the top edge of the
frame, as a symbol of life itself.

Klimt fitted his horse and rider perfectly into the square picture plane, but
deliberately cut off the top of the helmet. The balance of the composition is enhanced
by the golden band at the base. Parallel to it runs a narrow strip of flowering meadow,
in contrast to Dürer's stony terrain. The horizontal plane is emphasized, more strongly
than in Dürer's print, by the snake and by the horse's hindquarters and front leg,

Fig. 3
ALBRECHT DÜRER
Knight, Death and the Devil
Engraving, 1513, 9¾in by 7½in (24.6cm by 19cm)

Fig. 4
A suit of armour made for Emperor Maximilian I by Lorenz
Helmschmied, Augsburg, *circa* 1480–85
Reproduced courtesy of the Waffensammlung,
Kunsthistorisches Museum, Vienna

while in the vertical plane the lance and the three tree-trunks take over this function. The position of the horse's legs diverges from Dürer's work, but is similar to that in his *Small horse* of 1505.

Dürer's horseman refers back to one of his watercolour drawings, now in the Albertina, where an inscription identifies the armour as a contemporary German suit. In Klimt's painting the armour is different. The figure wears a combination of elements from three of the noblest fifteenth-century armours, one Italian and two German, all of them from the Waffensammlung of the Kunsthistorisches Museum in Vienna.

The director of this collection, Dr Ortwin Gamber, has identified the pieces: the helmet, pauldrons, vambraces and tassets derive from the armour of Roberto da San Severino, made in Milan, *circa* 1480; the breastplate is that of Emperor Maximilian I by Lorenz Helmschmied, Augsburg, *circa* 1480–85 (Fig. 4); and the legs are from another suit by Lorenz Helmschmied, made for Archduke Sigismund, *circa* 1485. The stirrups, spurs and bridle have been painted in Gothic style, but the dagger, lance and saddle were freely invented by the artist.

Sigismund's armour served as the model for the whole of the *Wohlgerüstete Starke* in the *Beethovenfries*, with the exception of the helmet, which is again that of Roberto da San Severino. This helmet, with its diamond pattern, must have had a special fascination for Klimt. His only adaptation was to replace the stars on the original with dots. He also used it for the Gorgons in the *Beethovenfries;* for Justitia in *Jurisprudenz*, one of the *Fakultätsbilder* (1903); in the portrait of Fritza Riedler (1906); and for his monogram on the cover of each instalment of the publication *Das Werk Gustav Klimts* (1914).

In contrast to Dürer's animal, Klimt's black horse appears strangely two-dimensional and the mane and tail have been treated very ornamentally. The painting also gives the impression that the rider is not holding the animal by the reins. Together with the mysterious gold background shining through the foliage, this produces an otherworldly and dreamlike effect. Klimt had undertaken a journey to Ravenna in the same year and his impressions, particularly of the gold mosaics, had a decisive influence on his work until about 1909.

The meaning of Dürer's picture has not been fully explained in 500 years, although most people have seen in it the Christian knight, steadfastly pursuing his course. It is equally difficult to state Klimt's intentions with certainty. In *Das Werk Gustav Klimts* (1914), the title is shown as *Das Leben ist ein Kampf*, 'Life is a struggle'. This is reminiscent of Friedrich Nietzsche's interpretation of Dürer's engraving as a 'symbol of our existence'. Klimt was clearly concerned to portray something universal as well, but his image can also be read in personal terms.

If we are to believe Alma Mahler, Klimt intended the *Wohlgerüstete Starke* in the *Beethovenfries* to be her husband, Gustav Mahler. This seems probable, considering his struggle for modern music and his efforts to interpret Beethoven. It has also been suggested that the figure represents Klimt himself; but such an interpretation can be applied much more reasonably to the *Goldene Ritter*.

Klimt's life was a struggle, against those who opposed his work, but even more a struggle with himself, constantly striving to achieve the highest perfection in his art. On this basis, it is possible to interpret the *Goldene Ritter* as a symbol of creative genius and its struggle with the outside world.

EMIL NOLDE
Women in a garden (*Flower garden*)
Signed and titled on the stretcher, 1915, 28¾in by 34⅝in (73cm by 88cm)
London £346,500($481,635). 26.VI.84

MAX BECKMANN
Women eating oysters
Signed and dated *A43*, 37½in by 21¾in (95.3cm by 55.3cm)
New York $275,000(£197,842). 15.V.84
From the collection of the Marion O. Hoffman Trust

GIACOMO BALLA
Screen
Pastel on canvas, 1918, height $71\frac{7}{8}$in (182.5cm)
Milan L140,120,000 (£59,880: $82,911). 11.IV.84

HENRY MOORE
Family group
Gouache, crayon and indian ink, signed, 1945,
19¼in by 15⅜in (48.9cm by 39.1cm)
New York $341,000 (£245,324). 17.XI.83

This is a study for a bronze family group of 1946.

Below
WASSILY KANDINSKY
Composition
Watercolour and brush and ink, *circa* 1917–18,
18⅝in by 34⅝in (47.3cm by 88cm)
London £165,000 ($229,350). 28.III.84

This watercolour was executed in Moscow.

The collection of Hélène Anavi

BALTHUS
Portrait of Hélène Anavi
Signed with initials and dated *1952*, 42½in by 35⅜in
(108cm by 89.8cm)
London £99,000($137,610). 27.III.84
From the collection of the late Hélène Anavi

The collection of Surrealist and post-war art formed by the late Madame Hélène Anavi was sold in London on 27 and 28 March 1984. An American, born in Beirut, she lived in France for many years. Upon her death in 1981, at the age of seventy-eight, she left instructions that her pictures should be auctioned by Sotheby's on behalf of the cancer research department at the Fondation pour la Recherche Médicale in Paris.

The collection was formed in Paris after the Second World War, according to her own excellent taste, but also with the advice of dealers, in particular Nina Dausset. Madame Anavi was involved in the artistic life of the city and bought many of her pictures directly from the artists, including six from the enigmatic Count Balthazar Klossowski de Rola, known as Balthus; among them was her own portrait (see above).

The collection contained seventeen works by Max Ernst, including the Surrealist *Monument aux oiseaux* (1927) and *La religieuse Portugaise* (1950) (see p. 117). There were also eighteen by Jean Dubuffet; the sitter for his portrait *Léautaud sorcier peau-rouge* was the writer and critic Paul Léautaud, editor of *Mercure de France*, a friend of Madame Anavi (see p. 116). Other artists represented were Joan Miró, Victor Brauner, Yves Tanguy (see p. 118), Christian Bérard, Dali, Matta and Wols (see p. 133).

In all the 159 lots sold for £4,665,595 ($6,485,177).

BALTHUS
La sortie du bain
Signed and dated *1957* on the reverse, 78¾in by 78¾in (200cm by 200cm)
London £847,000($1,177,330). 27.III.84
From the collection of the late Hélène Anavi

The recent Balthus retrospective at the Centre Pompidou in Paris and the Metropolitan Museum of Art, New York, focused particular attention on the six works by this artist in the sale, which alone made £1,849,100($2,570,249).

JEAN DUBUFFET
Léautaud sorcier peau-rouge
Signed on the reverse, 1946, 35½in by 28⅛in (90.2cm by 71.5cm)
London £143,000($198,770). 27.III.84
From the collection of the late Hélène Anavi

MAX ERNST
La religieuse portugaise
Signed and dated '50, 45⅝in by 35in (115.9cm by 88.9cm)
London £275,000 ($382,250). 27.III.84
From the collection of the late Hélène Anavi

YVES TANGUY
Genesis
Signed and dated *26*, 39$\frac{3}{8}$in by 31$\frac{7}{8}$in (100cm by 81cm)
London £148,500 ($206,415). 27.III.84
From the collection of the late Hélène Anavi

ALBERTO GIACOMETTI
The nose
Bronze with steel cage and wire, signed, numbered *3/6* and stamped with the foundry mark
Susse Fondeur, Paris, 1947, height of cage 32in (81.3cm)
New York $396,000 (£284,892). 16.V.84
From the collection of the Ratner family

FERNAND LEGER
Constructeurs avec arbre
Signed and dated *50*, and signed twice, dated *49* and *50* and titled *Les Constructeurs, Etude, Fragment d'en Haut, avec arbre* on the reverse, $42\frac{1}{2}$in by $54\frac{1}{4}$in (108cm by 137.8cm)
New York $616,000(£443,165). 15.V.84
From the collection of Nathan Cummings

JOAN MIRO
Woman and birds
Gouache and oil wash on paper, signed, and signed, titled and dated *Varengeville s/mer 13/iv/1940* on
the reverse, 15in by 18⅛in (38.1cm by 46cm)
London £407,000($565,730). 26.VI.84

This is the eighth in the series of twenty-three *Constellations* that Miró executed between January
1940 and September 1941, in France and Spain.

The collection of Serge Lifar

Three albums of material relating to productions of the Ballets Russes, 1910–14
London £148,500 ($206,415). 9.V.84
From the collection of Serge Lifar

This platinum print of Nijinsky in *L'Après-midi d'un faune*, 1912, was one of sixteen photographs by Baron de Meyer.

Serge Lifar joined Diaghilev's Ballets Russes in 1923 and became the last of the great principal dancers in the company. As Diaghilev's protégé and intimate friend, Lifar was at the master's deathbed in 1929.

Lifar's collection contained a wealth of material associated with the great days of the Ballets Russes. It featured décor and costume designs by many of Diaghilev's painter collaborators, among them Bakst, Ernst, Miró, De Chirico and Pruna. Picasso's Chinese Conjuror stood out among a number of fine costumes (see opposite); the artist's preliminary drawing was sold at Sotheby's last year (see *Art at Auction 1982–83*, p. 109). There were portraits by Picasso; music manuscripts by Debussy and Satie; many letters; Diaghilev's dressing case, complete with icon, and his bronze death mask, made at Lifar's instigation. Also included were three bound albums of contemporary photographs, autograph letters and other material, put together by the Marchioness of Ripon, documenting the early period of the Russian ballet (see above). Lady Ripon, a notable hostess and patron of the arts, was Diaghilev's earliest London sponsor and largely responsible for the début of his Russian ballet at Covent Garden in June 1911. Her daughter, Lady Juliet Duff, who backed Diaghilev's last two London seasons in 1928 and 1929, later presented these three volumes to Lifar. An autograph notebook with Diaghilev's plans for various ballets and performances is illustrated on p. 183.

The auction of 227 lots took place in London on 9 May 1984 and made in total £827,255 ($1,149,884).

PABLO PICASSO
Costume for the Chinese Conjuror in *Parade*, inscribed *1917 Leonid Massine and Leon Wojcikowski*
London £28,600($39,754). 9.V.84
From the collection of Serge Lifar and now in the Theatre Museum, Victoria & Albert Museum, London

Picasso's costumes and décor for Léonide Massine's ballet *Parade* marked the painter's début as a
designer for the stage.

BENJAMIN WEST, PRA
The death of General Wolfe
Oil wash, sepia ink and watercolour heightened with white, inscribed, 17in by 24in (43.2cm by 61cm)
New York $165,000 (£118,705). 30.V.84

This is the only known preparatory study for Benjamin West's *The death of General Wolfe*, probably for the original version of 1770, now in the National Gallery of Canada, Ottawa. James Wolfe died from wounds received during the successful British assault on Quebec, in 1759, and became a national hero in England. West departed from tradition in elevating this contemporary scene to the level of academic history painting, ennobling his subject by borrowing from traditional imagery of the Lamentation and the Deposition.

WILLIAM SIDNEY MOUNT
Any fish today?
Signed and dated *1857*, and titled on the reverse, 21¼in by 16¼in (54cm by 41.3cm)
New York $660,000 (£474,820). 8.XII.83

WILLIAM TROST RICHARDS
Mackerel Cove, Jamestown, Rhode Island
Oil on canvas mounted on masonite, signed and dated '94, 26¼in by 47in (66.7cm by 119.4cm)
New York $187,000 (£134,532). 30.V.84

THEODORE ROBINSON
Port Ben – Delaware and Hudson Canal
Signed and dated '93, 18in by 22in (45.7cm by 55.9cm)
New York $209,000(£150,360). 8.XII.83

A larger version of this painting is in the collection of the Pennsylvania Academy of the Fine Arts.

Opposite
JOHN FREDERICK KENSETT
Eagle Cliff, coast of Massachusetts
Signed with monogram and dated *1859*, 28½in by 45½in (72.4cm by 115.6cm)
New York $594,000(£427,338). 8.XII.83

THOMAS MORAN
The Grand Canyon
Signed and with artist's thumbprint, dated *1917*, 20in by 30in (50.8cm by 76.2cm)
New York $308,000 (£221,583). 8.XII.83

HENRY F. FARNY
On the move
Gouache on paper mounted on board, signed, with device, and dated *1901*,
11¾in by 18¼in (29.9cm by 46.4cm)
New York $220,000 (£158,273). 8.XII.83

FREDERIC REMINGTON
Coming to the call
Signed, *circa* 1905, $27\frac{1}{4}$in by $40\frac{1}{4}$in (69.2cm by 102.2cm)
New York $550,000 (£395,683). 30.V.84

GEORGIA O'KEEFFE
Pink pastelle
Pastel on linen, signed with initials and titled on the stretcher, 1924, 16in by 14in (40.6cm by 35.6cm)
New York $110,000 (£79,137). 8.XII.83

WOLS
Green streaked with black and red
Signed, 41in by 31⅞in (104.2cm by 81cm)
London £132,000 ($183,480). 27.III.84
From the collection of the late Hélène Anavi

YVES KLEIN
I. K. B. 234
Blue pigment on canvas laid down on panel, 1957, 29⅝in by 22in (75.2cm by 55.9cm)
London £57,200 ($79,508). 8.XII.83
From the collection of Madame Nicole Kugel

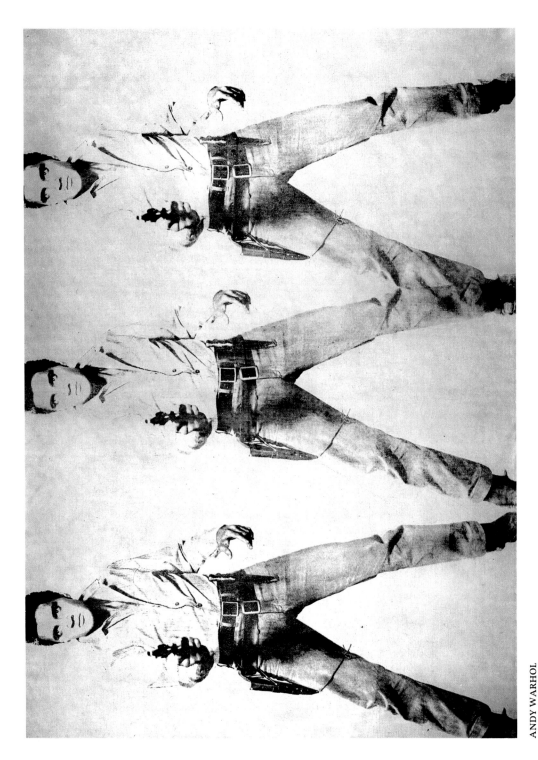

ANDY WARHOL
Triple Elvis
Acrylic silkscreened on canvas, *circa* 1962–64, 82in by 118in (208.3cm by 299.7cm)
New York $148,500(£106,835). 9.XI.83

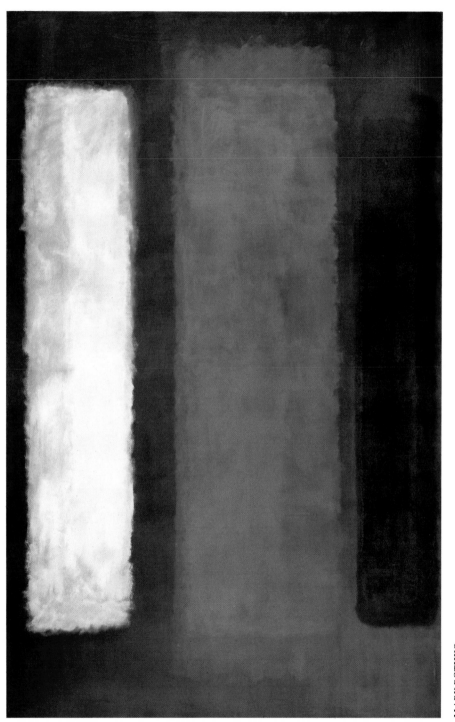

MARK ROTHKO
Black, maroons and white
1958, 102½in by 169in (260.4cm by 429.2cm)
New York $1,815,000 (£1,305,755). 9.XI.83
From the collection of Mr Ben Heller

ALEXANDER CALDER
Big crinkly
Mobile stabile, painted metal, signed, 1971, height approximately 288in (732cm)
New York $852,500(£613,309). 9.V.84
From the collection of the late Alfred Schmela

WILLEM DE KOONING
Bolton landing
Signed, 1957, 83¾in by 74in (212.8cm by 188cm)
New York $847,000(£609,353). 9.V.84
From the collection of the Inland Steel Co.

SAM FRANCIS
Untitled
1953, 79in by 56in (200.7cm by 142.3cm)
New York $363,000 (£261,151). 9.XI.83
From the collection of the late Robert Elkon

RICHARD DIEBENKORN
Ocean park no. 46
Signed with initials and dated *71*, 81in by 81in (205.8cm by 205.8cm)
New York $330,000(£237,410). 9.V.84

DIEGO RIVERA
The flower vendor
Oil on masonite mounted on panel, signed and dated *'41*, and inscribed on the reverse *Este cuadro lo pinto para Paulette Goddard, Diego Rivera en Mexico año de 1941*, 48in by 48in (121.9cm by 121.9cm)
New York $429,000 (£308,633). 29.V.84
From the collection of Paulette Goddard

FERNANDO BOTERO
The musicians
Signed and dated 79, 85½in by 74¾in (217.2cm by 190cm)
New York $242,000 (£174,101). 29.XI.83

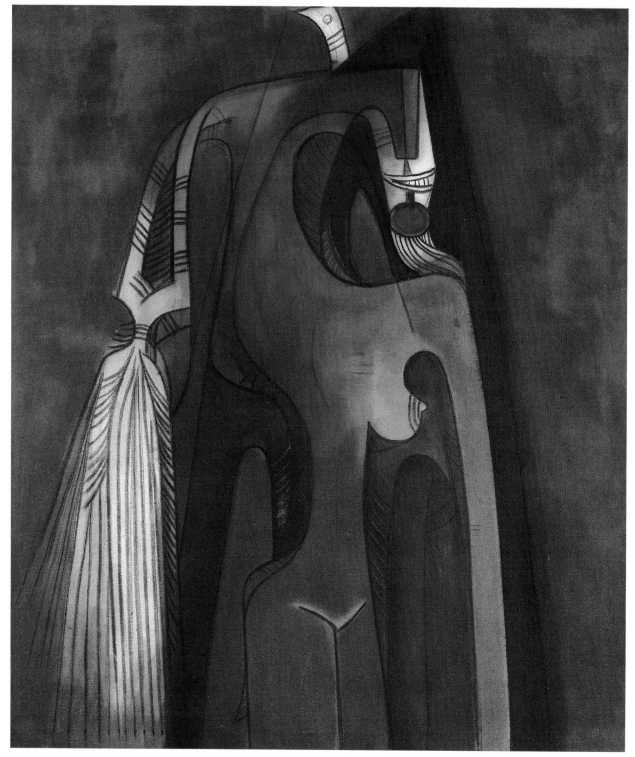

WIFREDO LAM
Water braids
1950, 49in by 43$\frac{1}{4}$in (124.5cm by 109.8cm)
New York $198,000 (£142,446). 29.V.84
From the collection of the late Joseph Cantor

FRIDA KAHLO
What the water gave me
Signed and dated *39*, 35¾in by 27¾in (90.8cm by 70.5cm)
New York $258,500(£185,971). 29.XI.83

Prints

QVANTVM FORMA FVGAX,QVANTVM VENVS IMPROBA POSSIT. EXEMPLO EST SOLIDI IVDICIVM PARIDIS.

GIORGIO GHISI
The judgement of Paris
Engraving after Giovanni Battista Bertani, 16½in by 21in (42cm by 53.3cm)
London £23,100 ($32,109). 6.XII.83

REMBRANDT HARMENSZ. VAN RIJN
Studies of the head of Saskia and others
Etching, an unrecorded early state, 1636, 6in by 5in (15.1cm by 12.6cm)
New York $29,700 (£21,367). 3.V.84

ODILON REDON
Dans le rêve
One of a set of ten lithographs on chine appliqué, 1879, sheet size $21\frac{1}{4}$in by $14\frac{1}{2}$in (53.7cm by 37cm)
London £68,200 ($94,798). 15.VI.84

This set constitutes the artist's first work in lithography. It was published in an edition of only twenty-five and very few complete sets are known.

FRANCISCO JOSE DE GOYA Y LUCIENTES
Los proverbios
One of a set of eighteen etchings with aquatint on wove paper, trial proofs, *circa* 1848,
sheet size $9\frac{7}{8}$in by $14\frac{3}{8}$in (25.2cm by 36.4cm)
New York $132,000(£94,964). 3.V.84

MARY CASSATT
The banjo lesson
Drypoint, soft ground and monotype printed in colours, on Vanderlay laid
paper, final state, signed in pencil and with the artist's monogram stamp,
circa 1893, 12in by 9¼in (30.4cm by 23.6cm)
New York $49,500 (£35,612). 3.V.84

WILLIAM BLAKE
Songs of Experience
Hand-coloured relief etching printed in brown on
wove paper, *circa* 1794,
$4\frac{3}{8}$in by $2\frac{3}{4}$in (11cm by 7cm)
London £10,450($14,526). 14.VI.84

This print was the frontispiece to Blake's *Songs of
Experience*.

HENRI DE TOULOUSE-LAUTREC
Idylle princière
Lithograph printed in colours on chine volant, signed in pencil, 1897,
sheet size 14⅞in by 10¾in (37.8cm by 27.4cm)
New York $55,000(£39,568). 2.V.84

The American heiress, Clara Ward, who married the Prince de Caraman-Chimay, is
seen here in a box with her gypsy lover, Rigo. The magazine *Gil Blas* of 9 January
1897 reported: 'the most heavily made up and artificial beauty among the American
ladies in Paris let herself be seduced by a certain pockmarked person who knows his
craft extremely well'.

EDVARD MUNCH
Angstgefühl
Lithograph printed in red and black on wove paper, trial proof, signed in pencil,
1896, 16¼in by 15⅜in (41.2cm by 39cm)
London £71,500 ($99,385). 7.XII.83

This is apparently a proof impression, aside from the edition of 100 printed for Ambroise
Vollard and published in 1896. The composition closely follows the painting of the same
subject, executed in 1894 and now in the National Gallery, Oslo.

Photographs

Hornbeam leaf
Photogenic drawing on paper bearing the monogram *N*, probably sensitized by Nicolaas Henneman, *circa* 1840–45, $4\frac{1}{2}$in by $5\frac{7}{8}$in (11.5cm by 14.8cm)
London £660($917). 29.VI.84

This photogenic drawing is one of a group of seven similar studies, which formed part of a series of photographs, prints and watercolours collected by Henry Bright (MP for Bristol, 1820–30) until his death in 1869.

DR HUGH DIAMOND
Elderly woman in bonnet holding dead bird
Albumen print, *circa* 1848–58, 7¾in by 5½in (19.7cm by 14.1cm)
London £9,350($12,997). 29.VI.84

Dr Diamond became superintendent of the Surrey County Asylum in 1848 and made various photographic studies of his patients. His work culminated in the presentation before the Royal Society in May 1856 of a paper: *On the application of Photography to the Physiognomy and Mental phenomena of Insanity*. Diamond's work represents one of the earliest uses of photography as a medium of scientific instruction.

EUGENE ATGET
Etang de Corot, Ville-d'Avray
Arrowroot print, numbered in the negative, titled and with photographer's studio
stamp on the reverse, *circa* 1900–10, 6$\frac{7}{8}$in by 9in (17.5cm by 22.9cm)
New York $15,400(£11,079). 9.XI.83

CHARLES SHEELER
Wheels
Silver print, signed on the mount, 1939, 6¼in by 9½in (15.9cm by 24.2cm)
New York $67,100 (£48,273). 9.XI.83
Now in the Detroit Institute of Arts, Michigan

There are only four known prints of this subject, a steam locomotive at Harmon, New York. It was taken in connection with the painting *Roller power*, now in the collection of Smith College, Northampton, Massachusetts.

Opposite
EDWARD STEICHEN
Nude with narcissi
Platinum print, signed and dated 1902, 6in by 7¾in (15.2cm by 19.7cm)
New York $23,100 (£16,619). 8.V.84

Steichen gave this photograph to a young American doctor, a supporter of the Photosecessionist movement, who treated him at the American hospital in Neuilly, Paris, during 1902.

Manuscripts and printed books

St Sebastian, one of two full-page miniatures on vellum by Simon Bening, cuttings from a Book of Hours, Bruges, *circa* 1520–30
London £35,200 ($48,928). 3.VII.84
Now in the J. Paul Getty Museum, Malibu

The Adoration of the Magi, one of two full-page miniatures on vellum, cuttings from a psalter, Würzburg, *circa* 1240
London £176,000 ($244,640). 3.VII.84
From the collection of the late Lord Clark of Saltwood, OM, CH, KCB, and now in the J. Paul Getty Museum, Malibu

Sixteen other miniatures from this exceptionally grand psalter cycle are known, all in the British Library. Lord Clark's medieval and Renaissance illuminated miniatures were from the collection of the Scottish antiquary James Dennistoun (1803–55), an early disciple of the Gothic revival and one of the first connoisseurs of the Italian primitives. He bought the Würzburg cuttings in Munich in 1839.

The Gospel Book of Henry the Lion

Christopher de Hamel

Last December, the long-lost Gospels of Henry the Lion sold to Quaritch and Kraus for £8,140,000, the highest price ever paid at auction for a work of art (Figs 1–2, 4–5 and frontispiece). It is probably the first time since the Renaissance that a book has become a more expensive work of art than any painting. The almost anonymous twelfth-century artist-monk of Helmarshausen Abbey, brother Herimann, has been thrust into the glare of giant prices, ahead of Leonardo, Rembrandt and Turner. However, sums hailed as records one year are soon toppled and manuscripts will certainly sell for more than £8 million some day; the Book of Kells would make more now.

Sotheby's first wrote to the curator of Henry the Lion's Gospel Book in 1933 (Fig. 3), offering to include it in a sale, but at the onset of the Depression could it have matched the amazing £15,400 paid for the manuscript of *Alice in Wonderland* at Sotheby's in 1928? In the English-speaking auction arena of the 1920s, white rabbits had more appeal than German lions. It is fascinating to look back at some of the record prices that created sensations in their own time.

In the eighteenth century, the fashion was for Renaissance elegance. A sixteenth-century psalter, ascribed then to Giulio Clovio, made £169 1s at the Duchess of Portland's sale in 1786: it was resold at Sotheby's in 1981 for £140,000. The record, however, probably lay with a dainty volume by the seventeenth-century scribe Nicolas Jarry: this made 14,510 livres (about £725) at the Duc de la Vallière's sale in 1783. It might make only ten times that price today; a book by the same scribe went for £3,000 at Sotheby's in July 1978 and was not cheap. The absolute block-buster of Georgian taste, however, was the Valdarfer Boccaccio, a sophisticated Italian Renaissance printed book, which stunned the bibliographical world by selling for £2,260 at the Roxburghe sale in May 1812. There are several contemporary descriptions of the auction, which opened at a hundred guineas and edged up in bids of £10: 'You might have heard a pin drop,' wrote Dibdin. 'All eyes were turned – all breathing well nigh stopped.'

It is doubtful whether Henry the Lion's Gospels would have made even a few hundred pounds at auction in 1812. The great Irish Gospels, the Book of Armagh, were unsold at £390 in 1831. The Alcuin Bible was bought-in at £1,500 without a single bid in April 1836. A tenth-century Gospel Book achieved only £89 in the Tite sale in 1874. Not until the 1880s did collectors' taste really turn to northern Europe.

Fig. 1
The Gospel Book of Henry the Lion, *The dedication miniature*, one of forty-one full-page miniatures, ten full-page carpet pages or interlaced initials and over 1,500 illuminated initials, from a manuscript on vellum, illuminated by the monk Herimann, Helmarshausen Abbey, Lower Saxony, *circa* 1175–80
London £8,140,000 ($11,314,600). 6.XII.83
Now in the Herzog-August-Bibliothek, Wolfenbüttel, Lower Saxony

The Gospel Book was commissioned by Henry the Lion, Duke of Saxony and Bavaria, for presentation to Brunswick Cathedral.

Fig. 2

The Scourging of Christ; The Crucifixion

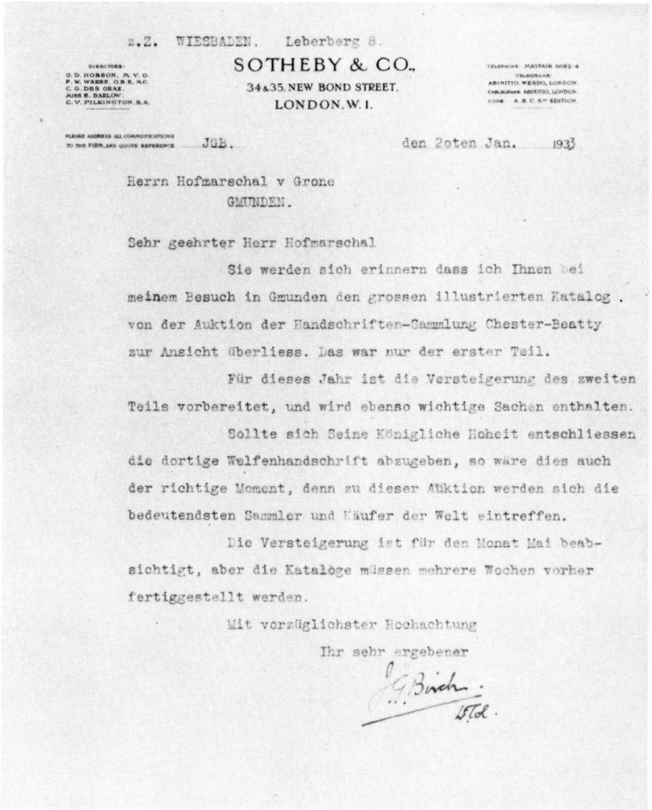

z.Z. WIESBADEN. Leberberg 8.

DIRECTORS:
G.D. HOBSON, M.V.O.
F.W. WARRE, O.B.E., M.C.
C.G. DES GRAZ.
MISS E. BARLOW.
C.V. PILKINGTON, B.A.

SOTHEBY & CO.,
34 & 35, NEW BOND STREET,
LONDON, W.1.

TELEPHONE: MAYFAIR 0082-4
TELEGRAMS: ABINITIO, WESDO, LONDON
CABLEGRAMS: ABINITIO, LONDON
CODE: A B C 5th EDITION

PLEASE ADDRESS ALL COMMUNICATIONS TO THE FIRM, AND QUOTE REFERENCE JGB.

den 2oten Jan. 1933

Herrn Hofmarschal v Grone
GMUNDEN.

Sehr geehrter Herr Hofmarschal

Sie werden sich erinnern dass ich Ihnen bei meinem Besuch in Gmunden den grossen illustrierten Katalog . von der Auktion der Handschriften-Sammlung Chester-Beatty zur Ansicht überliess. Das war nur der erster Teil.

Für dieses Jahr ist die Versteigerung des zweiten Teils vorbereitet, und wird ebenso wichtige Sachen enthalten.

Sollte sich Seine Königliche Hoheit entschliessen die dortige Welfenhandschrift abzugeben, so wäre dies auch der richtige Moment, denn zu dieser Aüktion werden sich die bedeutendsten Sammler und Käufer der Welt eintreffen.

Die Versteigerung ist für den Monat Mai beabsichtigt, aber die Katalöge müssen mehrere Wochen vorher fertiggestellt werden.

Mit vorzüglichster Hochachtung
Ihr sehr ergebener

Fig. 3
A letter from Sotheby's to Hofmarschal von Grone, dated 2 January 1933, sent with a copy of the first sale catalogue of Sir Alfred Chester Beatty's illuminated manuscripts, asking whether the Gospels of Henry the Lion might be offered for sale.

The twelfth-century Ottobeuren Sacramentary made a little under £1,000 at Sotheby's in 1887. The Hamilton Palace Purple Gospels made £1,500 to Quaritch in 1889, a lot of money for a book with no pictures. The printed Mainz Psalter of 1457 was taken up to £4,950 in the Syston Park sale in 1884, 'at which, after calling this enormous price three times, Mr Hodge raised his hammer for the last time and sealed the purchase of the famous codex to Mr Quaritch at this unprecedented price amid the loudest applause ever heard in this room.'

The glamour of this price was soon obsolete. The first five-figure manuscript was the Hours of Jeanne of Navarre, which Quaritch bought on commission at Sotheby's in 1919 for £11,800. At a quick rule-of-thumb calculation of 10 percent a year compound interest, this is approximately equal to £7,470,000 now, uncannily close to the hammer price of the Henry the Lion Gospels. By July 1929, the record had moved to £33,000 (the Bedford Hours, again to Quaritch) and, thirty years later, had edged to £65,000 (the Dyson Perrins Apocalypse) and then 1,000,000 francs (the Rothschild Apocalypse sold in Paris, in 1968), £370,000 (the Spinola Hours in 1976) and £770,000 (the Ottobeuren Sacramentary in 1981). All the last four were bought by Mr H. P. Kraus, three of them at Sotheby's.

What raised the Gospels of Henry the Lion to more than ten times the previous highest price for a medieval illuminated manuscript and well over the highest price for any painting to date? First of all, there was the importance of the original

Fig. 4
The Dance of Salome; The Decollation of St John the Baptist

Fig. 5
The Calling of the Apostles; St John the Baptist Preaching in the Wilderness

Fig. 6

provenance. The manuscript was illuminated for Henry the Lion (*circa* 1129–95), Duke of Saxony, Duke of Bavaria, conqueror and crusader, ruler of unbelievable wealth, founder of Munich and cousin of Emperor Frederick Barbarossa. In February 1168, Henry married Matilda, elder daughter of Henry II of England (sister, therefore, of Richard the Lion Heart and King John). Henry and Matilda are depicted twice in the manuscript, once kneeling before the patron saints of Brunswick (Fig. 1) and, a second time, being crowned by God in the company of as many regal and imperial relations as they could muster between them. The picture is of English interest, in that it includes a contemporary portrait of Henry II and one of the earliest depictions of St Thomas Becket, martyred at the instigation of Henry II in 1170. Even now, Henry the Lion is regarded as one of the great heroes of German chivalry and this is the only surviving book certainly made for him.

Secondly, the manuscript created something of a sensation simply because it had been lost for nearly fifty years. It was bought from Prague Cathedral in 1861 by the last king of Hanover and his descendants still owned it in 1933, when Sotheby's wrote to ask if there was any chance of the book being sold. After the Second World War, it was offered for sale secretly (both the British Museum and the Pierpont Morgan Library turned it down) and acquired by a group, who never declared their identity or its whereabouts. Part of the aura of the manuscript was certainly due to its blazing reappearance after half a century of darkness.

Even the name of Henry the Lion is romantic. In 1959, Sotheby's sold the Peter Lombard, made in 1166 for Henry's ally, Hartwig, Bishop of Bremen, 'saxonie autem ducatum regente heinrico', says its colophon, but there is no magic in that name. The

Fig. 7

appellation 'the Lion' conjures up pleasing images of knighthood and distant antiquity. Sotheby's had one enquiry from an American zoo, who evidently supposed that Henry the Lion was a famous animal.

Finally, and most of all, the manuscript was valuable because of its pictures. It is folio in size, 13½in by 10in, and has forty-one full-page pictures of amazing complexity in brilliant colours, silver and gold. It forms a complete art gallery of Romanesque painting. When he ordered the manuscript, Henry the Lion had just returned from the Holy Land and Byzantium, where he had been entertained by the emperor at Easter 1172, and this is a key document for the reception of Byzantine art into northern Europe. We know where the manuscript was illuminated, at Helmarshausen Abbey, about sixty-five miles south-west of Brunswick, and even the name of the artist, Herimann, which appears in the dedication inscription in gold uncials. Such precise information is exceedingly rare for any Romanesque work of art, especially one of such extravagant quality. On the basis of this book, eighteen other manuscripts and fragments have been ascribed to the Helmarshausen scriptorium in the second half of the twelfth century, but the Gospel Book of Henry the Lion far exceeds them all in grandeur and importance.

The bidding for lot 50 on 6 December opened at £1 million and went up in increments of £100,000 and £200,000 to £7,400,000. The sale lasted two and a quarter minutes (Figs 6–7). The great book was bought at last by a consortium on behalf of the West German government. On 11 January 1984 a camouflaged military aeroplane was sent from Berlin especially to collect it; at about three in the afternoon the manuscript arrived back in Lower Saxony, the dukedom of Henry the Lion.

Book of Hours, *The Crucifixion*, one of twenty-one full-page miniatures from a manuscript in Dutch on vellum, illuminated by the Master of Guillebert de Mets, southern Netherlands, *circa* 1430–50, made for the Augustinian nunnery of Bethany, near Malines, Belgium
London £220,000 ($305,800). 3.VII.84

Book of Hours, *The Betrayal*, one of fifty-eight miniatures from a manuscript on vellum, illuminated by the Master of the Geneva Latini, Rouen, *circa* 1460–75
London £330,000 ($458,700). 6.XII.83

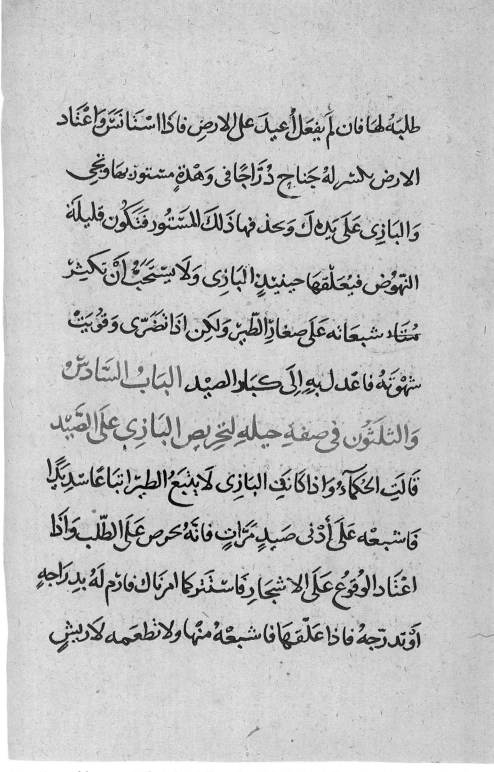

A treatise on falconry, attributed to Adham ibn Muhriz al-Bahili, an Arabic manuscript in *naskh* script, probably Syria, a near contemporary copy of a version dated 1223
London £31,900 ($44,341). 16.IV.84

Portrait of a Persian lady of the court at Isfahan by Muhammad Qasim al-Tabrizi,
signed, Isfahan, *circa* 1640–50
London £27,500 ($38,225). 16.IV.84

An Ottoman *firman* of Sultan Mustafa II in *diwani* script, dated 1695
London £3,520 ($4,893). 2.VII.84

Shah Abbas receiving the Mughal ambassdor Khan 'Alam in 1618 by Bishan Das, a page from a
Mughal royal album, inscribed in *nasta'liq* script *'amal-i-Bishan Das, circa* 1625
London £30,800($42,812). 17.X.83

Godly and necessarye Prayers, 1549
London £16,500 ($22,935). 26.VII.84

The book is illustrated slightly smaller than actual
size; it is the only recorded copy of the earliest
known English book to have been printed in
miniature format. It contains neatly written notes
by Robert Spencer, 1st Baron Spencer of
Wormleighton, about members of his family.

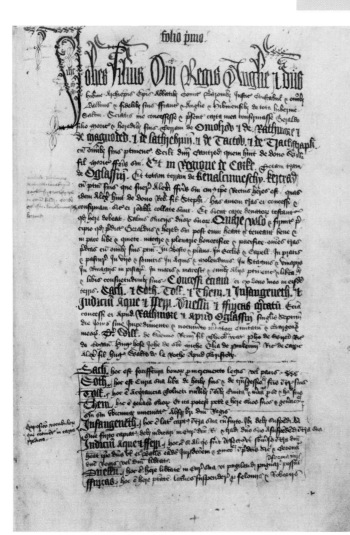

The Red Book of the Earl of Kildare, transcripts of
documents relating to the family and Irish
estates of the Earls of Kildare from medieval
times onwards, in Latin and English, on vellum,
compiled by Philip Flattisbury, approximately
155 pages, 1503 and later
London £25,300 ($35,167). 17.VII.84
From the collection of the Duke of Leinster

Gerald, 8th Earl of Kildare, who ruled Ireland
almost continuously from 1477 to 1513, gave
orders for the compilation of this book in 1503.
It was clearly intended as a comprehensive
record of the Kildare estates. Philip Flattisbury
also served under the 9th Earl, compiling a
chronicle of Ireland for him in 1517, now lost.

NICOLAUS HOGENBERG
The Procession of Clement VII and Charles V after the Coronation at Bologna, 1530, forty hand-coloured engraved plates, signed and dated by the scribe *Jehan Ruchie Gantois prestre en lan MDXXXII,* Antwerp, 1532
London £27,500($38,225). 17.XI.83

A collection of natural history books and atlases

The collection of natural history books and atlases sold on 1 February 1984 was the finest of its kind to be offered at auction since the Second World War. It was distinguished by the criteria employed in its formation: namely, to obtain the finest copies of some of the greatest colour-plate books ever produced. It would now be virtually impossible to assemble a collection of this quality.

The age of the great natural history colour-plate books extends from the early eighteenth to the late nineteenth century, when chromolithography and, later, photography replaced the earlier techniques of engraving and colouring by hand, and printing in colour. It was an age in which exploration, first-hand observation and scientific classification evoked an unprecedented interest in natural phenomena among educated society, both in Europe and America.

The discovery and description of new species inspired the production of large and expensive folios, profusely illustrated by the best artists of the day, designed to appeal to prevailing tastes in collecting. The most popular of these books were undoubtedly those devoted to birds and flowers, although other subjects were widely covered.

Of the bird artists, the magnificent plates engraved by Robert Havell for Audubon's mammoth undertaking, *The Birds of America* (1827–38), remain unsurpassed (see opposite). John Gould employed Edward Lear, Joseph Wolf and others in the production of 3,000 hand-coloured lithographed plates for the splendid series of volumes that he published over some fifty years, depicting birds, many of them newly discovered, from various parts of the world.

In the field of botanical illustration, Pierre-Joseph Redouté developed a method of printing in colours from a single stipple-engraved plate, with washes and highlights added by hand, to produce the softness and brilliance of a watercolour. His *Les Roses* (1817–24) (see p. 176) and *Les Liliacées* (1802–16), like the birds of Audubon, remain pinnacles of artistic achievement.

Among a number of atlases and travel books in last February's sale, perhaps the finest atlas was Ottens's composite *Atlas van Vytegezogte Landkaarten* (see p. 177). It provides a good illustration of the kind of mapping available to the collector of means in the eighteenth-century Netherlands. David Roberts's and Louis Haghe's *The Holy Land, Syria, Idumea, Arabia; Egypt & Nubia* is a magnificent example of tinted lithographic printing (see p. 177); the work was one of the most important and elaborate ventures in nineteenth-century publishing.

In total, the sale of 59 lots realized £2,260,060 ($3,141,483).

JOHN JAMES AUDUBON
The Birds of America, four volumes, first edition, 435 hand-coloured etched plates
with engraving and aquatint by W. H. Lizars and Robert Havell, Junior, after
Audubon, published by the author, London, 1827–38
London £1,100,000 ($1,529,000). 1.II.84

Rosa Gallica Aurelianensis   *La Duchesse d'Orléans.*

P. J. Redouté pinx.   Imprimerie de Rémond   Langlois sculp.

PIERRE-JOSEPH REDOUTE
Les Roses, three volumes, first edition, large paper copy, 170 etched plates after Redouté, printed in colour and finished by hand, bound in purple half morocco by Simier, Paris, 1817–24
London £74,800 ($103,972). 1.II.84

REINER and JOSUA OTTENS
Atlas van Vytegezogte Landkaarten, two engraved titles, four engraved allegorical frontispieces and eighty-five maps and plates by seventeenth and eighteenth-century map-makers and others, hand-coloured and heightened with gold, Amsterdam, *circa* 1730. London £96,800($134,552). 1.II.84

DAVID ROBERTS, RA
The Holy Land, Syria, Idumea, Arabia; Egypt & Nubia, six volumes, six hand-coloured lithographed titles and 241 hand-coloured lithographed plates by Louis Haghe after David Roberts, London, 1842–49. London £85,800($119,262). 1.II.84

JOHANNES BLAEU
Atlas Major, sive cosmographia blaviana, eleven volumes, first complete edition, nine engraved frontispieces and 597 hand-coloured engraved plates, Amsterdam, 1662
London £55,000 ($76,450). 1.XII.83

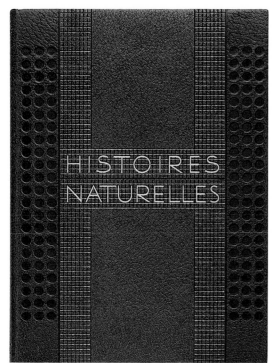

JULES RENARD
Histoires naturelles, twenty-two lithographed plates, five original sketches and one original drawing in coloured crayon by Henri de Toulouse-Lautrec, later olive green morocco binding by Georges Cretté, Paris, 1899
Monte Carlo FF721,500 (£62,091 : $85,995). 24.VI.84
From the collection of the late Florence J. Gould

Opposite
GEORGE CATLIN
North American Indian Portfolio, twenty-five hand-coloured lithographed plates, London, 1844
London £26,400 ($36,696). 22.V.84

XAVERIO MANETTI, LORENZO LORENZI and VIOLANTE VANNI
Ornithologia methodice digesta atque iconibus aeneis ad vivum illuminatis ornata, five volumes, five engraved frontispieces and 600 hand-coloured engraved plates, Florence, 1767–76
London £44,000 ($61,160). 19.VII.84
From the collection of the late Finn Salomonsen

ABRAHAM LINCOLN
An autograph telegram to his wife, one page, City Point,
Virginia, 2 April 1865
New York $48,400 (£34,820). 26.X.83
From the collection of the Utica Public Library,
New York

This is one of Lincoln's last letters to his wife, in which he
tells her of events leading up to General Grant's victory
in northern Virginia. They were reunited on 6 April and
he was assassinated eight days later.

Opposite
ALBERT EINSTEIN
The autograph manuscript of his paper 'Einheitliche
Feldtheorie und Hamiltonsches Prinzip', seven
pages, 1929
New York $38,500 (£27,698). 25.IV.84
From the collection of Dr John D. Stanitz

This is the final draft of a major paper on
'Unified Field Theory'.

DECLARATION OF INDEPENDENCE
Autograph material by each of the signatories,
thirty-four signed autograph letters, eleven signed
autograph documents, seven signed documents, three
signed letters and one signature cropped from a book,
eighteen of revolutionary war date, seven dated 1776
New York $209,000 (£150,360). 26.X.83
From the collection of the New Jersey Historical Society

21

Einheitliche Feldtheorie und Hamilton'sches Prinzip.
Von A. Einstein   (Diese Berichte 1929, I)

In einer vor Kurzem erschienenen Abhandlung habe ich ohne Zugrundelegung eines Variations-Prinzipes Feldgleichungen für eine einheitliche Feld-Theorie aufgestellt. Die Berechtigung dieser Feldgleichungen ruht auf der Voraussetzung der Kompatibilität der 16 Feldgleichungen (10) *loc. cit.* Da es nicht gelang zwischen diesen Gleichungen oder identische Relationen herzustellen, haben die Herren Lanczos und Müntz begründete Zweifel an der Zulänglichkeit der dort gegebenen Feldgleichungen geäussert, (ohne dass hierüber bisher eine klare Entscheidung vorliege.) Unterdessen fand ich, dass es möglich ist, das Problem in völlig befriedigender Weise unter Zugrundelegung eines Hamilton-Prinzipes zu lösen, wobei die Vereinbarkeit der Gleichungen untereinander von vornherein feststeht. Die in der früheren Arbeit abgeleiteten Identitäten sowie die dort gebrauchten Bezeichnungen werden hier benutzt bezw. übernommen.

§ 1. Allgemeines über das Hamilton'sche Prinzip, angewandt auf ein Kontinuum mit Riemann-Metrik und Fern-Parallelismus.

Es sei $\mathfrak{H}$ eine skalare Dichte, welche sich aus den $g_{\mu\nu}$ und h_{μ}^{α} algebraisch ausdrückt. Dann gehören zu dem Hamiltonschen Prinzip

$$\delta\left\{ \int \mathfrak{H}\, d\tau \right\} = 0, \quad \cdots (1)$$

in welchem nach den h_{μ}^{ν} variiert wird, die Feldgleichungen

$$\mathfrak{g}^{\mu\alpha} = \mathfrak{H}^{\mu\alpha} - \left(\mathfrak{H}_{\underset{2}{\mu\nu}} \right)_{/\nu} = 0, \quad \cdots (2)$$

wobei die Grössen $\mathfrak{H}^{\mu\alpha}$ und $\mathfrak{H}_{\underset{2}{\mu\nu}}$ durch die Gleichungen

$$\left.\begin{aligned} \mathfrak{H}^{\mu\nu} &= \frac{\partial \mathfrak{H}}{\partial g_{\mu\nu}}\\[2mm] \mathfrak{H}_{\underset{2}{\mu\nu}} &= \frac{\partial \mathfrak{H}}{\partial h_{\mu}^{\nu}} \end{aligned}\right\} \quad (3)$$

ELIZABETH BARRETT BROWNING
The autograph working notebook for *The Seraphim, and other Poems*, 159 pages, *circa* 1835–37
London £20,900 ($29,051). 16.VII.84

The Seraphim, and other Poems (1838) was the first adult work that Elizabeth Barrett Browning issued under her own name. In writing to her friend John Kenyon she claimed that 'with all its feebleness and shortcomings and obscurities', it was 'the first utterance of my own individuality'. The discarded texts and heavy revisions in this notebook afford a detailed study of her artistic development.

Opposite
IGOR STRAVINSKY
The autograph manuscript of *Renard*, vocal score, signed and dated twice *1916*, 151 pages
New York $88,000 (£63,309). 14.XII.83

This was one of a group of manuscripts given by the composer to his wealthy Chilean patroness Madame Eugenia Errazuriez. She had met Stravinsky in May 1914, during the first Madrid performance of the *Firebird*, and paid him a stipend of 1,000 francs a month for the last two years of the First World War. Madame Errazuriez was also a friend of John Singer Sargent and Picasso.

SERGE DIAGHILEV
An autograph working notebook containing plans for ballets and performances between 1926 and 1929, approximately 140 pages
London £46,200 ($64,218). 9.V.84
From the collection of Serge Lifar

Mahler's First Symphony

Stephen Roe

'Well! My work is finished! Now I should like to have you by my piano and play it to you! . . . It has turned out so overwhelming, it came gushing out of me like a mountain torrent! This summer you shall hear all of it! All of a sudden all the sluice-gates in me opened! Perhaps one of these days I shall tell you how it all happened!' Thus Gustav Mahler triumphantly announced the completion of the first version of his First Symphony to his friend, Friedrich Löhr, in early 1888.[1] But this extraordinary work, perhaps the most original and accomplished 'first symphony' by any composer since Berlioz's *Symphonie Fantastique*, was not yet complete. Mahler subjected it to a series of revisions and alterations, which continued even beyond the publication of the first edition in 1899. Mahler's first conception was of a gigantic symphonic poem in two parts, comprising five movements. For a performance in Hamburg in 1893, the work was retitled *Titan, eine Tondichtung in Symphonieform* and each movement was given a descriptive title. By 1896, after a further revision, the work was titled *Symphonie*, the second movement 'Blumine' had been discarded and a four-movement plan without titles adopted. This version became definitive in the first edition.

The resulting textual problems posed by the surviving manuscripts and editions of the symphony have never been satisfactorily discussed by Mahler scholars. Many questions will undoubtedly be answered, and a few new ones raised, by the discovery of a previously unknown manuscript, sold at Sotheby's on 10 May 1984 (Fig. 1). This discovery is a major event for Mahler scholarship. The manuscript is important, not only for what it tells us about the early history of the First Symphony, but also for the light it sheds on Mahler's working methods as a whole.

This full score, together with copies of ten early songs from the set known as *Lieder und Gesänge aus der Jugendzeit* in the same sale, is predominantly in the hand of an amanuensis, one 'F. Weidig'. Mahler subjected the manuscript to extensive and rigorous revision. Twenty-two pages are completely autograph: the title page, boldly inscribed 'Symphonie Nro I von Gustav Mahler' (the 'M' of the surname altered, after the composer had absent-mindedly begun writing 'Gustav' again); the first seventeen pages of the first movement (the Introduction and opening bars of the exposition), loosely inserted, the corresponding scribal pages cut out; three pages in the Finale (two pasted over Weidig's version); and a page of supplementary instructions in blue pencil on the fly-leaf. In the scribal parts of the manuscript, Weidig's attractive and

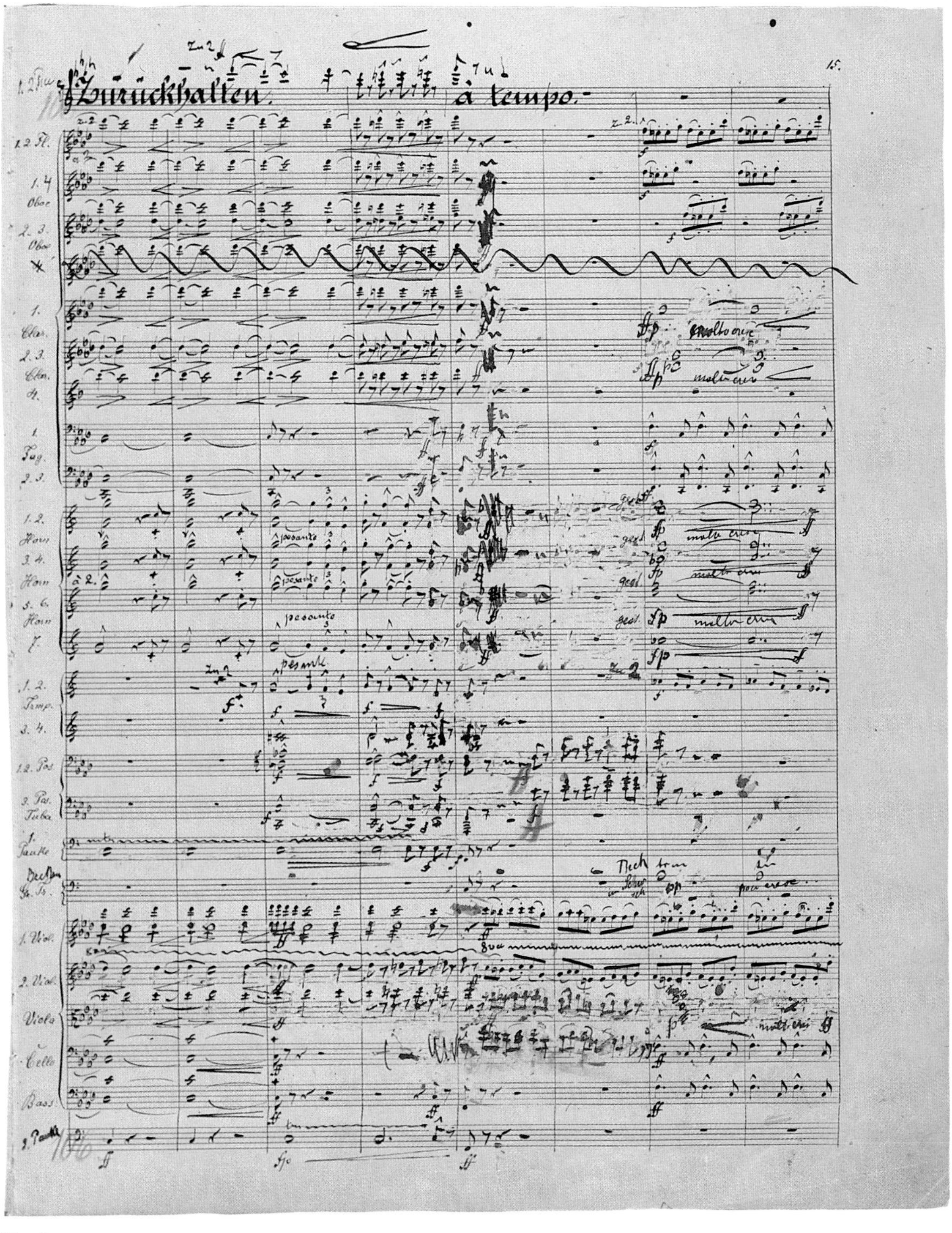

Fig. 1
GUSTAV MAHLER
A manuscript of the First Symphony in D major, 206 pages, twenty-two autograph, the remainder
extensively revised and annotated by the composer, *circa* 1896–99
London £143,000 ($198,770). 10.V.84

Fig. 2
An autograph page from the manuscript

meticulous hand is subjected to unremitting assault by Mahler with black and red ink, and blue and red pencil. Only two pages, in a manuscript of over two hundred, remain unscathed.

Mahler makes no major structural alterations. 'Blumine' has already gone and otherwise not a bar is added or subtracted. The composer thoroughly revises the orchestration, often scratching out Weidig's script (in most cases the original is still legible) and adds his new ideas, either directly on the existing staves, or on newly drawn lines above or below the main systems. Mahler's aim here was to effect a thoroughgoing revision of textures. This is conceived not just as a thinning down or thickening of the instrumentation, but often as a complete rethinking of the orchestral balance. He further seeks to clarify his intentions to the conductor and performer: the score bristles with dynamic marks, precise tempo indications, new injunctions and instructions in the composer's hand. The most radical is his request that the horn players should stand for the peroration in the Finale: 'Alle Hornisten *stehen auf* um die möglichst grösste Schallkraft zu erzielen'. There are commands too for Weidig, from which it would seem that Mahler intended him to produce yet another copy of the score.

This raises the questions: how many pre-publication manuscripts were there and where does this score come in the chronology? There must have been at least four manuscripts of the symphony. Two manuscripts of the five-movement version survive. The autograph (sold at Sotheby's, 8 December 1959), now in the Osborn Collection, Yale University, apparently dates from 1888 but was revised by Mahler in 1893.[2] Another copy, in a hand that can now be identified as Weidig's, in the New York Public Library, is also annotated by Mahler, although less spectacularly than the new manuscript. It is tentatively dated to between 1893 and 1896 by Donald Mitchell.[3]

The present manuscript, dating from between *circa* 1896 and 1899, is the missing link between the five and four-movement versions. 'Blumine' has evidently just been removed. The 'ghost' of this movement survives in the manuscript: there is a break in rehearsal numbers (which run continuously throughout the symphony) between no. 33, at the end of the first movement, and no. 47, at the beginning of the *Ländler*. Nos 34–46 belonged to 'Blumine'. The manuscript is close, but not identical, to the text published by Weinberger in 1899. It is unthinkable that this working manuscript should have been used as the *Stichvorlage*. It must be assumed that *another* manuscript was copied later (presumably by Weidig), from which the engraver prepared the plates of the first edition.

It is clear from the manuscript that the creation of the distinctive Mahlerian sounds and textures was gradually rather than spontaneously achieved. Mitchell's remark of the third movement, that 'one of Mahler's most innovatory sound-worlds . . . was precisely imagined from the outset'[4] (that is, in 1888 or 1893), surely needs reappraisal in the light of the new evidence. In this manuscript Mahler adds new instruments in the Funeral March, including cor anglais, bass clarinet and two extra horns; the two parts for E flat clarinets (according to Mitchell, only one was scored in the 1888–93 version)[5] are written here in C by Weidig, then altered to E flat by Mahler. These and many other alterations and refinements, such as the addition of fifth, sixth and seventh horns throughout most of the first movement, are surely introduced as a result of Mahler's experience with the vast orchestral forces of the Second Symphony, completed in 1894 and performed in 1895 and 1896. Most interesting of all is Mahler's difficulty with the opening of the first movement. This magical introduction, perhaps the most original touch in the entire work, took him eleven years to perfect. There are three versions of it in the two previously known manuscript sources; in the new manuscript the composer cuts out Weidig's transcription of what is possibly a fourth version. Mahler's replacement is close to the first edition (1899), but differs in the division of the double basses and in some of the instructions for the fanfares.

Mahler's half-promise to Löhr to explain how the First Symphony came into being seems never to have been fulfilled. In any case, it would only have been part of the story. Much of the rest is found in this new manuscript.

NOTES
1. *Selected Letters of Gustav Mahler*, ed. K. Martner (1979), pp. 111–12
2. D. Mitchell, *Gustav Mahler: The Wunderhorn Years* (1975), pp. 196 ff.
3. Op. cit., p. 204
4. Ibid., p. 214
5. Ibid., p. 212

Coins and medals

The Polar medal and Royal Geographical Societies' medals awarded to Captain Lawrence Oates,
6th Inniskilling Dragoons
London £55,000 ($76,450). 28.VI.84

These Polar medals were awarded posthumously to the legendary hero of Captain Scott's ill-fated
second Antarctic expedition of 1910–13. Dispirited by losing the race to be first to the South Pole and
beset by appalling weather conditions on their return journey, the British party perished. Crippled by
frostbite, Oates had walked out into a blizzard so that his comrades might travel more quickly without
him, but his self sacrifice proved to be in vain.

    The auction also contained an identical group awarded to Lieutenant Henry 'Birdie' Bowers, RIM,
another member of Scott's Polar team, which, by an astonishing coincidence, emerged for sale at the
same time from a different and unconnected source.

An official badge for a
Lady of the Bedchamber to
HM Queen Alexandra, given to
the Dowager Countess of Morton
on Coronation Day,
9 August 1902
London £4,620 ($6,422). 1.III.84

The St Paul's Cathedral
George Cross group awarded to
Lieutenant Robert Davies, RE
London £16,000 ($22,240).
13.X.83

On 13 September 1940,
Lieutenant Davies was in charge
of a party detailed to recover a
one-ton bomb that had fallen in
the vicinity of St Paul's Cathedral
the previous night. The bomb,
8ft in length and buried 27ft 6in
underground, was extracted with
great difficulty and driven by
Lieutenant Davies personally to
Hackney Marshes for detonation.
As the *Sapper* magazine reported
at the time, 'The Cathedral would
have undoubtedly been razed to
the ground had the bomb . . .
exploded.'

FRIESLAND, eagle rijksdaalder
struck in gold, 1584
Amsterdam DFl46,400
(£10,867:$15,065). 18.V.84

BRABANT, double florin of Albert
and Isabella struck in gold, 1602
Amsterdam DFl23,200
(£5,433:$7,532). 18.V.84

KINGDOM OF THE NETHERLANDS,
proof 2½ gulden struck in gold
of William III, 1874
Amsterdam DFl30,160
(£7,063:$9,792). 17.V.84

HOLLAND, piedfort rijksdaalder,
depicting William the Silent, 1584
Amsterdam DFl10,208
(£2,391:$3,314). 18.V.84

GRONINGEN, piedfort rijksdaalder,
1561
Amsterdam DFl10,904
(£2,554:$3,540). 18.V.84

INDEPENDENT STATES OF BRABANT,
piedfort daalder, 1584
Amsterdam DFl20,880
(£4,890:$6,779). 18.V.84

Left and right
FRIESLAND, large
koggerdaalder struck in
gold, 1652
Amsterdam DFl51,040
(£11,953:$16,571).
18.V.84

Koggerdaalders were
struck on special
occasions throughout the
seventeenth century,
presumably for
presentation purposes.

The gold and silver coins of the Netherlands illustrated on this page are from the Virgil M. Brand Collection.

Left
UNITED STATES OF AMERICA,
Assay Office of Gold,
50 dollars, 1852, San Francisco
provisional mint
London £5,280 ($7,339). 22.III.84

Right
ISLAMIC, Buwayhid Dynasty,
silver dinar of abu-Talib Rustam,
AH 387 (997 AD),
al-Muhammadiya mint
London £4,620 ($6,422). 17.IV.84

UNITED STATES
OF AMERICA,
half eagle, 1795
London £6,600
($9,174). 22.III.84

ROMAN, aureus of
Maximian Hercules,
289–90 AD
London £8,800
($12,232). 2.II.84
From the Virgil M.
Brand Collection

ENGLAND, gold pattern unite of Charles I,
by Nicholas Briot, 1630
London £9,900 ($13,761). 22.III.84

Left and right
RUSSIA, gold medal of the
Empress Elizabeth, 1754,
commemorating the
foundation of
Moscow University
London £1,155 ($1,605).
22.III.84

Arms and armour

A German morion, *circa* 1600, height 13in (33cm)
London £37,400 ($51,986). 1.XI.83
From the collection of the late John F. Hayward

The quality of etching on this helmet is typical of both Brunswick and Saxony, but the style suggests
the former.

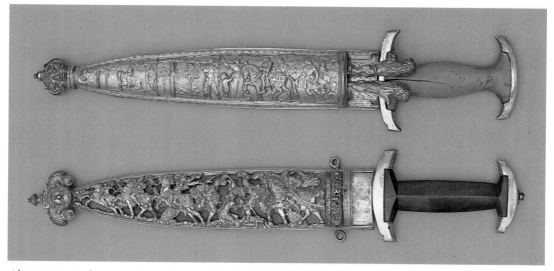

Above A Swiss dagger with gilt-brass sheath, cast and chased with the story of William Tell, *circa* 1570, length 16¼in (41.3cm). London £28,600 ($39,754). 15.V.84
Below A Swiss dagger with gilt-brass sheath, cast, chased and pierced with the Judgement of Trajan, sixteenth-century style, length 16¾in (42.6cm). London £6,050 ($8,410). 15.V.84

From left to right
A Saxon sword, late sixteenth century, length 42in (106.7cm). £7,700 ($10,703)
A Saxon rapier, late sixteenth century, length 48in (121.9cm). £9,350 ($12,997)
A Saxon garniture of rapier and dagger, late sixteenth century, length of rapier 50in (127cm), length of dagger 16in (40.7cm). £14,300 ($19,877)

These weapons are from the collection of the late John F. Hayward and were sold in London on 1 November 1983. They were all formerly in the armoury of the Electors of Saxony at Dresden.

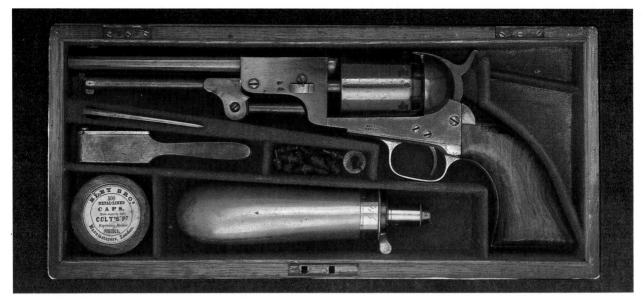

A Hartford Dragoon percussion cap revolver by Samuel Colt, length 13½in (34.3cm), *circa* 1853–56
London £9,900 ($13,761). 31.VII.84

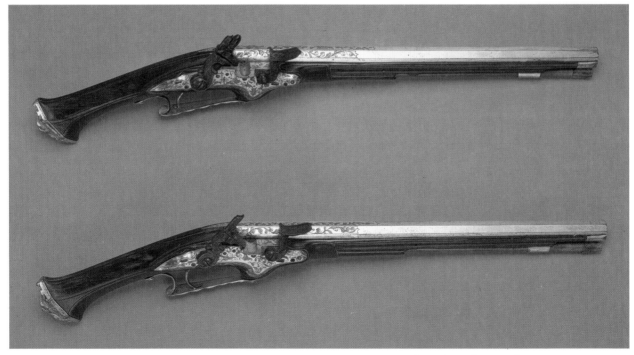

A pair of Swiss flintlock pistols mounted with hard-brass octagonal barrels, attributed to Felix Werder,
Zurich, *circa* 1630, length of barrels 12⅞in (32.7cm)
New York $46,200 (£33,237). 3.III.84

Felix Werder worked in Zurich as a goldsmith and gunmaker. He was celebrated in his own time for
fine pistols, which were often intended for presentation. Werder seldom used his mark, so it is not
unusual for this pair of pistols to be unsigned.

Above, from left to right
A $2\frac{5}{8}$-in 1896-pattern bronzed-brass 'Perfect'
trout reel by Hardy. London £1,155 ($1,605). 2.V.84
A $2\frac{1}{2}$-in 1891-pattern brass 'Perfect' trout reel
by Hardy. London £3,630 ($5,046). 2.V.84
Below, from left to right
A Bouglé lightweight trout reel by Hardy,
circa 1910, diameter of drum $2\frac{1}{4}$in (5.7cm)
London £990 ($1,376). 2.V.84
A St George Tournament fly reel by Hardy, 1938,
diameter $3\frac{1}{4}$in (8.3cm). London £660 ($917). 2.V.84

A garniture of db 12-bore assisted opening round-action ejector sporting guns by David McKay Brown,
engraved by Malcolm Appleby, serial numbers 801, 802 and 803, 1982,
length of barrels 27in (68.6cm)
Gleneagles £24,200 ($33,638). 29.VIII.83

Works of art

A bronze aquamanile in the form of a unicorn, probably Lower Saxony, *circa* 1300, height 10⅝in (27cm)
London £82,500 ($114,675). 1.XII.83

Only three other unicorn aquamaniles are known.

A Limoges enamel and copper-gilt eucharistic dove from the Marienstift at Erfurt, *circa* 1200, height 7½in (19cm)
London £176,000 ($244,640). 1.XII.83

This dove was sold in the von Hirsch sale, 22 June 1978, for £100,000. It is known to have been in the monastery at Erfurt, West Germany, from an eighteenth-century watercolour drawing in the Bibliothèque Nationale, Paris, which was prepared on the instructions of the Elector Lothar Franz von Schonborn, Archbishop of Mainz, for the antiquary Dom Bernard de Montfaucon.

A French Romanesque limestone capital, mid-twelfth century, height 15½in (39.4cm)
London £20,900 ($29,051). 3.IV.84
Now on loan to the Victoria & Albert Museum, London, from a private collection in New York

A Tyrolean Romanesque wood figure of Christ Crucified, *circa* 1200, height 19in (48.3cm)
London £44,000 ($61,160). 3.IV.84
From the collection of Dr Peter Hierzenberger

A French Gothic limestone group of the Virgin and Child, last quarter fourteenth century,
height 18½in (47cm)
London £37,400($51,986). 1.XII.83

A Styrian Gothic polychrome pine figure of a female saint, second half fourteenth century,
height 42⅛in (107cm)
London £33,000 ($45,870). 3.IV.84
From the collection of Dr Peter Hierzenberger

The collection of
Thomas F. Flannery, Jr

A French enamelled gold commesso, set with chalcedony and rock crystal, depicting Prudence, *circa* 1550–60, height 2$\frac{1}{4}$in (5.7cm)
London £88,000 ($122,320). 1.XII.83
From the collection of the late Thomas F. Flannery, Jr

The collection of the late Thomas F. Flannery, Jr (1926–80), was sold in London on 1 and 2 December 1983. He had run a family business in Chicago and been actively involved in the civic affairs of that city. His passion for collecting began after the Second World War, culminating in a magnificent collection of medieval and later works of art. His first interests were the mechanism of clocks and gemstones, particularly coloured varieties, which he learned to polish and mount with skill. During the 1950s his scope broadened, influenced by his taste for vivid colours and delicate workmanship, and the nucleus of the collection was formed. He relied largely upon the great dealers in Europe and America, who contributed much to his growing knowledge of the minor arts. A scholarly approach to provenance became an intrinsic part of his connoisseurship and he shared his collection willingly with a steady stream of serious students in the field.

The collection was rich in enamels, metalwork, jewels, wood carvings and ivories. Some of these are illustrated on the following pages. One of Flannery's rare early clocks is discussed elsewhere in an article by George Daniels (see p. 224) and a Roman rock-crystal amphoriskos is illustrated on p. 352.

In all the sale of 526 lots made £2,180,812 ($3,031,329).

A Limoges enamel and copper-gilt châsse, *circa* 1200, height 8½ in (21.6cm)
London £66,000 ($91,740). 1.XII.83
From the collection of the late Thomas F. Flannery, Jr

A gilt-bronze group of the Virgin and
Child, France or the Netherlands,
circa 1420, height 4½in (11.5cm)
London £132,000 ($183,480). 1.XII.83

Right
A Lower Saxon gilt-bronze figure of
St Thaddeus, *circa* 1350, height 13in (33cm)
London £165,000 ($229,350). 1.XII.83

According to tradition, this figure was
formerly in the Hohenzollern-Sigmaringen
Collection. It is one of eight surviving
gilt-bronze figures from a retable.

Opposite
Left A Hungarian silver-gilt and
cloisonné-enamel chalice, second quarter
fifteenth century, height 8¼in (21cm)
London £13,200 ($18,348). 1.XII.83
Right A Hungarian silver-gilt and
cloisonné-enamel chalice, by Nicholas
Cynowec, inscribed and dated 1462,
height 8¼in (21cm)
London £22,000 ($30,580). 1.XII.83

The works of art on these pages are
from the collection of the late
Thomas F. Flannery, Jr

Left
A South German jewelled and enamelled cast and chased gold lion pomander, inscribed *CHE. GIRE. ANCOR* and on the back *QUIS. OGGI. ORNA.*, *circa* 1575, height 2¾in (7cm)
London £60,500($84,095). 1.XII.83
From the collection of the late Thomas F. Flannery, Jr

Below
Two views of a jewelled and enamelled gold pendant cross, Augsburg, late sixteenth century, height 4½in (11.4cm)
London £52,800($73,392). 1.XII.83
From the collection of the late Thomas F. Flannery, Jr

The objects on this page were formerly part of the crown jewels of Portugal, inherited in 1920 by Nevada, Princess of Braganza, widow of Prince Alfonso, Duke of Oporto, second son of King Luis I. A pendant cross of this design is worn by Maria of Austria, daughter of Emperor Charles V, in a portrait by Antonio Moro, now in the Prado, Madrid.

A Sicilian copper-gilt and coral holy-water stoop,
mid-seventeenth century, height 18in (45.7cm)
London £11,550 ($16.055). 3.IV.84

A Paduan bronze oil lamp attributed to the workshop of
Andrea Riccio, early sixteenth century, height $5\frac{1}{2}$in (14cm)
London £42,900 ($59,631). 4.VII.84

A French bronze study of a horse, attributed to the workshop of Antoine Coysevox, *circa* 1680, length $33\frac{7}{8}$in (86cm)
Monte Carlo FF2,442,000 (£210,155:$291,061). 25.VI.84

A boxwood figure of Christ Crucified, probably South Germany, second half seventeenth century,
height 20½in (52.1cm)
New York $22,000(£15,827). 2.III.84

A Byzantine icon of the Triumph of Orthodoxy, first half fifteenth century,
15¼in by 12¼in (39cm by 31cm). London £22,000 ($30,580). 15.II.84

Opposite
A Cretan icon of St Onouphrios the Great by Emmanuel Lambardos, signed, first quarter
seventeenth century, 21⅞in by 14⅜in (55.5cm by 36.5cm). London £41,800 ($58,102). 1.VI.84

A Fabergé gold, nephrite and enamel table clock in the form of a compass rose, workmaster
Mikhail Perchin, St Petersburg, *circa* 1890, width 5¼in (13.3cm)
New York $60,500(£43,525). 14.XII.83

This clock was designed for use aboard the Imperial yacht *Polar Star*.

Opposite
Part of the Kremlin Service, 195 pieces, each marked with the cypher of Nicholas I
or Alexander II, Imperial Porcelain Manufactory, St Petersburg, 1837– 38
London, total £97,900($136,081). 15.II.84

The service was commissioned by Emperor Nicholas I for the Grand Kremlin Palace, which
was rebuilt at this period in a new 'national style' based on Byzantine and old Russian models.
The decoration is to designs by Professor Teodor Solntsev, who took his inspiration from
seventeenth-century metalwork; the pattern of the dessert plates can be traced to a gold plate
made for Tsaritsa Natalia Kirilovna.

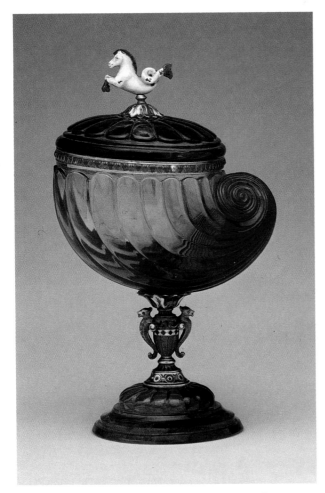

A Fabergé gold, enamel and smoky quartz standing cup and cover, workmaster Mikhail Perchin, St Petersburg, 1899–1903, height $4\frac{5}{8}$in (11.7cm)
Geneva SFr 49,500 (£15,815: $21,903). 17.V.84

This is one of the few Historismus pieces by Fabergé.

A Swiss jewelled, gold and enamel automaton and watch, *circa* 1810–20, height $3\frac{1}{2}$in (9cm)
Geneva SFr 88,000 (£28,115: $38,938). 17.V.84

An enamel snuff box, Augsburg, *circa* 1750, width $2\frac{1}{2}$in (6.5cm)
Geneva SFr 12,650 (£4,042: $5,597). 17.V.84

The views on the top and bottom of this box are taken from early eighteenth-century engravings. The lid shows Augsburg town hall and St Peter am Perlach. The skating scenes on the sides can be dated with some certainty to the mid-eighteenth century by the style of the skates, which are fitted with long spikes.

A jewelled, gold and enamel musical singing-bird box with watch, maker's mark of Jean-Georges
Rémond & Cie, Geneva, *circa* 1820, width 3¾in (9.5cm)
Geneva SFr 82,500 (£26,358: $36,504). 17.V.84

A gold and hardstone snuff box with applied bands of fluted cornelian over red lacquer, Dresden,
circa 1770, width 3⅛in (8cm)
Geneva SFr 115,500 (£36,901: $51,106). 16.XI.83

A gold and enamel *boîte à portrait*, inset with a miniature of Antoine Vitré by Jacques Bordier, signed and dated *1651*, maker's mark of Jean-Baptiste Fossin & Fils, Paris, *circa* 1852, width 3¼in (8.4cm) Geneva SFr93,500(£29,872:$41,372). 17.V.84

Jean-Baptiste Fossin & Fils served as jewellers to the crown during the reign of Louis-Philippe (1830–48). A letter dated June 1852 from Anatole Demidoff, Prince of San Donato, confirms his commission of this box for the price of about 2,500 francs. Antoine Vitré was director of the royal press under Louis XIV.

A three-colour gold and enamel snuff box, maker's mark of Charles le Bastier, Paris, 1768, width 2¾in (6.8cm)
Geneva SFr63,800(£20,383:$28,230). 16.XI.83

A jewelled, gold and enamel *boîte à miniatures*, inset with miniatures by van Blarenberghe, signed, maker's mark of Pierre-François Drais, Paris, 1777–78, width 3⅜in (8.5cm)
Geneva SFr 264,000 (£84,345: $116,814). 16.XI.83

The miniature on the lid shows a celebrated royal hunt at Compiègne in 1740, when a stag stood at bay on the roof of a cottage; the other panels are also on the theme of hunting. This box belonged to Louis XVI.

A diamond, two-colour gold and enamel snuff box, maker's mark of Jean Formey, Paris, 1768, width 3½in (9cm)
Geneva SFr 242,000 (£77,316: $107,080). 16.XI.83

EDWARD NORGATE

Above, left Mary Harrison, *circa* 1630, $2\frac{1}{8}$in (5.5cm). £28,600 ($39,754)

Above and below, right John Harrison, Junior, *circa* 1622, $2\frac{1}{8}$in (5.5cm), and his coat of arms, dated *1622*, $2\frac{1}{2}$in (6.4cm). £33,000 ($45,870)

Below, left Judith Norgate, after Isaac Oliver, *circa* 1613, 2in (5.1cm). £27,500 ($38,225)

These miniatures from the collection of Miss Mary Lawson-Tancred were sold in London on 5 July 1984.

The versatile Edward Norgate (*circa* 1580–1650) was at various times a tuner of the king's virginals, organs and other instruments; a writer and illuminator of royal letters; Windsor Herald and Clerk of the Signet. His surviving miniatures are few, but they are finely executed and he wrote two important treatises on the art of limning. This group of portraits demonstrates borrowings from the style of both Hilliard and Oliver. John and Mary Harrison were man and wife; the armorials may once have formed the back of an original case for his miniature.

JOHN SMART, JUNIOR
The Hon. Edward Lygon, watercolour on paper, signed and dated *1806*, 3⅞in (9.9cm)
London £3,740 ($5,199). 12.III.84

The Hon. Edward Lygon was the youngest son of the 1st Earl Beauchamp. He was a colonel in the
13th Light Dragoons, and cornet and sub-lieutenant in the 2nd Life Guards. He died on 11 November
1860. The style of this miniature is close to that of John Smart, Senior, the painter's father and master.

Judaica

Hymns and blessings for the marriage ceremony according to the Italian rite, Abraham and the messenger,
Abraham and the king, two of sixty full-page miniatures from a manuscript in Hebrew, on vellum,
signed in monogram, possibly illuminated by Conrad Meyer, Italy, mid-seventeenth century
New York $297,000 (£213,669). 1.II.84
From the collection of Mr Sigmund Harrison

The Mannerist style of the illustrations suggests a familiarity not only with artists such as Pontormo or
Rosso Fiorentino, but also with earlier masters like Michelangelo and Raphael.

A Polish jewelled parcel-gilt silver Torah crown, with niello inscription in Hebrew recording the makers Moshe ben Reb Yosef SGL and Gedalya ben Reb Yitzchak, dated 1796, height 10½in (26.7cm) New York $88,000(£63,309). 27.VI.84

Unlike most towns in western Europe, where guild regulations effectively excluded Jews from the making of silver until after the Napoleonic wars, Jews were permitted to work in silver in Poland. However, they remained outside the guilds and therefore without recorded maker's marks. The Hebrew inscription on this crown circumvents Polish regulations by recording what the guild marks would have set out.

Clocks and watches

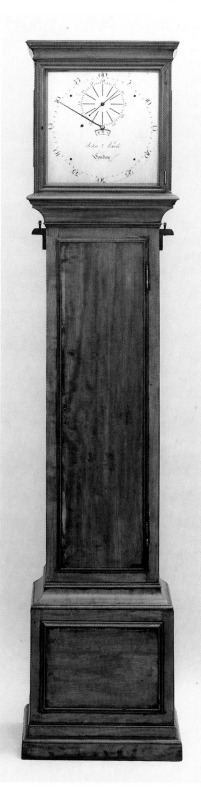

Left
A mahogany month regulator by
John Arnold, London, *circa* 1785,
height 6ft 4in (193cm)
London £27,500 ($38,225). 27.X.83
From the collection of
Dr D. B. Doran

Right
A walnut month longcase clock by
Daniel Quare, London, *circa* 1705,
height 8ft 4in (254cm)
London £18,700 ($25,993). 7.VI.84
From the collection of
R. I. R. Dean, Esq.

An ebony pendulum clock by Ahasuerus Fromanteel, London, *circa* 1660, height 7¾in (19.7cm)
London £46,200 ($64,218). 27.X.83
From the collection of Benjamin Bass, Esq.

This is the third earliest known English pendulum clock, a hitherto unrecorded example, which was recognized by an expert on a routine visit to the West of England.

Spring-driven clocks of the middle ages

George Daniels

It is not known who made the first mechanical clocks. Their construction would require a knowledge of mechanics and mathematics, as well as practical experience with tools. In the Middle Ages scientific knowledge was almost the prerogative of the Church and it is probable that the first clocks were made in and for the monasteries.

The earliest references to such clocks are in the first half of the fourteenth century, so the turn of the thirteenth century would be a likely date for their realization. These clocks were driven by a weight suspended from a rope wound around a drum. The falling weight turned the wheels, whose speed of rotation was controlled by an escapement. The escapement consisted of a toothed wheel engaging a pivoted, dumb-bell bar to cause it to rock on its pivots and allow one tooth of the wheel to pass at each oscillation. The escapement is the great invention that made the clock possible but, again, its origins are unknown. Perhaps it was the adaptation of a known mechanism, such as a spit for turning meat at a steady speed before the fire.

By the middle of the fourteenth century, the heavy iron mechanism had been developed to strike the passing hours on a bell and, installed in the church tower, served to remind the populace of the hours of prayer. Very soon after this, small chamber clocks are recorded and these would have been fixed to the wall in a room of a private house. The clocks were costly to make and were found in only the best houses. Few could afford more than one, so the timekeeper was confined to a single room. The clock as a domestic servant had become a reality and, from the middle of the fourteenth century, the professional clockmaker was established.

It was not until the end of the fifteenth century that the invention of the mainspring as a substitute force for gravity allowed the construction of portable clocks that could keep going while being carried from room to room. The spring was a ribbon of hard hammered brass or steel, contained in a barrel with a loose spindle. With one end of the spring attached to the inside wall of the barrel and the other end attached to the spindle, the spring could be tensioned by turning the spindle. The resultant energy would turn the barrel to drive the wheels of the clock. The spring exerted adequate force when fully wound, but this diminished steadily as the spring unwound with the passing hours. This had a most depressing effect on the rate of timekeeping, which got slower and slower as the spring ran down. The solution to this debility was

Fig. 1
A French gilt-metal table clock with
alarum, stamped *BLOIS*, possibly early
sixteenth century, height $4\frac{1}{8}$in (10.5cm)
London £104,500 ($145,255). 1.XII.83
From the collection of the late
Thomas F. Flannery, Jr

the invention of the fusee. This spiral pulley of steadily increasing diameter is coupled to the barrel by a gut line so that, when fully wound, the greatest force of the spring is taken by the smallest diameter. As the spring runs down, so the gut travels along the increasing diameter to equalize the diminishing power and maintain a more uniform rate of timekeeping. By this means the clocks were capable of indicating time to about half an hour fast or slow each day. This is poor by today's standards, but was undoubtedly a quantum leap in portable timekeeping for the period.

Allowing that the escapement had been invented without publicity in an earlier age, the invention of the mainspring and fusee stand as the greatest horological inventions of this early period, and elevated the art to a science. Yet no one claimed their invention, nor do contemporary chroniclers mention any names, although clocks containing fusees and mainsprings are described. The most diligent researches by generations of students have failed to discover their origins.

Thus it is that the little clock from the Flannery Collection, sold in London last December (Figs 1–2), is a rare and elegant example of a great horological mystery. On the underside of the base it is enigmatically stamped *BLOIS*, so its place of origin is known. The simplicity of the case, devoid of decoration except for the piercing of the frieze for the bell chamber, indicates an early date, certainly by the first quarter of the sixteenth century. Although Blois was a focus of royal patronage, it was not significant as a horological centre, as Versailles was to be at a later date. Such clocks were made in many parts of France with slight differences of mechanism or decoration, depending on the place of origin. Some strike the hours in passing, some have striking and alarum, and others, like the Flannery clock, have alarum only. Except for the general change from iron to brass for the movements and more fanciful decoration for the cases, they show no sign of development from some recognizable, primitive form. They simply appear as fully developed domestic clocks in the earliest days of portable spring-driven timekeepers.

The earliest documentary evidence for the existence of the spring-driven clock is from 1482 and makes reference to Italian examples; but there are no known survivors. The earliest dated spring-driven clock is owned by the Society of Antiquaries in London. It was made by Jacob the Czech in 1525 and is quite different from the little Blois clock, both in size and style of construction. At $9\frac{3}{4}$ inches diameter and 5 inches high it dwarfs the Blois piece, which measures about $4\frac{1}{8}$ inches high by 3 inches. They represent different schools, whose only common feature is their function.

Contemporary with the Czech clock and the Blois clock, an industry flourished in South Germany. The Czech example is similar in style to the German examples, in the form of a flat drum with the dial on the top surface and, since there was no established Czech industry, it was presumably influenced by German work.

However, while the Blois clock may be described as primitive, the German clocks are crude. It is all a question of subtlety of style and the finish of the components. Perhaps the French makers saw the ticking, measurer of eternity as a thing of independent existence, and endowed it with a dignity and elegance that reflected their pleasure in the timelessness of craftsmanship. Peter Henlein, who is said to have made the first German spring-driven clocks, was a locksmith and, if it were he who influenced the German craftsmen, this might account for the somewhat unimaginative

Fig. 2
Detail of the clock, showing the
mechanism

impression of functional mechanics. This is in direct contrast to the architectural
grace of the little French hexagonal tower cases.

Germany is generally credited with being the first in the field of portable clocks,
followed by the French. The main evidence for this would seem to be the absence of
any identifiable earlier French examples. As we have seen, the earliest reference to a
portable clock mechanism is Italian. The French clocks are more Italian than German
in their style and feeling for delicate craftsmanship. Thus it may be that the French
learned from the Italians. Certainly the early French clocks are more sophisticated
than the contemporary German pieces and display advanced workmanship to produce
a better-quality mechanism. Some noted modern historians are of the opinion that
the little Blois clock could be as early as 1480. In this case it would add weight to the
theory that the oldest surviving spring-driven clocks are not German but French.

Above, from left to right

ROBERT MOLYNEUX NO. 738
A gold, enamel and pearl cased verge watch, London, *circa* 1800, diameter 2in (5.1cm)
London £1,650 ($2,294). 23.II.84

ALEXANDER CUMMING NO. 765
A gold and enamel cased dumb quarter-repeating cylinder watch and châtelaine, London, 1769,
diameter 1⅞in (4.9cm). London £5,500 ($7,645). 23.II.84

RALPH GOUT NO. 4565
A gold and enamel pair-cased quarter-repeating duplex watch, bearing the cypher of Catherine
the Great, London, 1793, diameter 2⅜in (5.9cm). London £3,850 ($5,352). 23.II.84

Below, from left to right

A gold and enamel cased verge watch in the form of a heart, inscribed *Breguet à Paris, circa* 1800,
length 3⅜in (8.6cm). London £4,620 ($6,422). 23.II.84

RICHARD CLARKE NO. 2527
A gold, enamel and pearl cased verge watch and fob, London, *circa* 1800, diameter 2⅛in (5.4cm)
London £5,720 ($7,951). 23.II.84

ILBERY NO. 1061
A gold, enamel and rose-diamond set centre seconds pair-cased cylinder watch, London,
circa 1800, diameter 2⅜in (5.9cm). London £6,600 ($9,174). 23.II.84

THOMAS TOMPION NO. 99
An ebony quarter-repeating bracket clock, London, *circa* 1690, height 12½in (31.8cm)
London £34,100 ($47,399). 7.VI.84

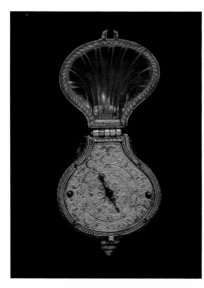

A gilt-metal and rock crystal cased
scallop-shell verge watch
by A. Blampignon, Lyons,
early seventeenth century,
length $1\frac{7}{8}$in (4.8cm)
New York $26,400(£18,993). 4.VI.84

Right
A gold, enamel and pearl cased
openface sweep-seconds quarter-
repeating watch for the Oriental
market, possibly by Piguet &
Meylan, no. 1425, *circa* 1800,
diameter $2\frac{1}{4}$in (5.7cm)
New York $42,900 (£30,863).
4.VI.84
From the collection of
Mrs John G. Love

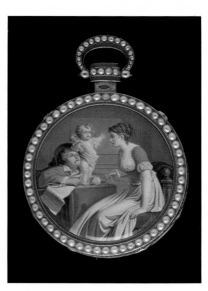

Left
EDWARD PRIOR NO. 16838
A gold and enamel triple-cased
quarter-repeating watch for the
Turkish market, London, *circa* 1790,
diameter $1\frac{7}{8}$in (4.8cm)
New York $12,100(£8,705). 14.II.84

Left
CHARLES FRODSHAM
NO. 09587
A gold cased eight-day
fusee keyless pocket
chronometer,
London, 1915,
diameter $2\frac{7}{8}$in (7.2cm)
London £20,900
($29,051). 23.II.84

Right
DENT NO. 57114
A gold cased thirty-five
minute split-seconds
fusee keyless lever
karrusel, London, 1900,
diameter $2\frac{3}{8}$in (6cm)
Geneva SFr 36,300
(£11,597:$16,062).
16.XI.83

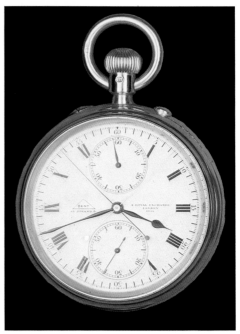

Above, from left to right
A gold Oyster day-date wristwatch by Rolex, *circa* 1974, diameter 1⅜in (3.6cm)
London £3,410 ($4,740). 12.IV.84
A gold Prince wristwatch by Rolex, *circa* 1930, length 1¾in (4.5cm)
London £1,320 ($1,835). 12.IV.84
A gold wristwatch by Cartier, 1963, diameter 1in (2.6cm)
London £2,200 ($3,058). 12.IV.84
A gold calendar wristwatch by Rolex, *circa* 1950, diameter 1½in (3.8cm)
London £3,740 ($5,199). 12.IV.84

Below, from left to right
A gold day-date Oyster wristwatch by Rolex, diameter 1⅜in (3.6cm)
London £3,190 ($4,434). 12.IV.84
A gold Prince wristwatch by Rolex, *circa* 1930, length 1⅝in (4cm)
London £3,520 ($4,893). 12.IV.84
A gold Prince wristwatch by Rolex, *circa* 1930, length 1⅝in (4cm)
London £1,925 ($2,676). 12.IV.84
A gold Mystery wristwatch by Vacheron & Constantin and Le Coultre, *circa* 1950,
diameter 1¼in (3.3cm). London £770 ($1,070). 12.IV.84

Musical instruments

A two-manual harpsichord by Jacob and Abraham Kirckman, London, 1779, inscribed *Jacobus et Abraham Kirkman Londini fecerunt 1779*, length 7ft 11in (241.5cm)
London £22,000 ($30,580). 25.XI.83

The 'Bonjour' violoncello by Antonio Stradivari, Cremona, *circa* 1690, labelled *Antonins Stradivari Cremonensis Faciebat Anno 168 ***, length of back 30in (76.2cm)
London £275,000 ($382,250). 5.IV.84

The 'Bucher' violin by Antonio Stradivari, Cremona, 1683, labelled *Antonius Stradiuarius Cremonensis Faciebat Anno 1683*, length of back 14in (35.6cm) London £101,200 ($140,668). 5.IV.84

A violin by Joseph filius Andrea Guarneri, Cremona, *circa* 1714, labelled *Joseph Guarnerius filius Andrea fecit Cremona sub titulo S. Teresia 1714*, length of back $13\frac{15}{16}$in (35.3cm) London £88,000 ($122,320). 5.IV.84

The 'Lyall' violin by Antonio Stradivari, Cremona, 1702, labelled *Antonius Stradivarius Cremonensis Faciebat Anno 1702*, length of back 14in (35.6cm)
New York $231,000 (£166,187). 18.I.84
From the collection of the late Mr Frank M. Kessler

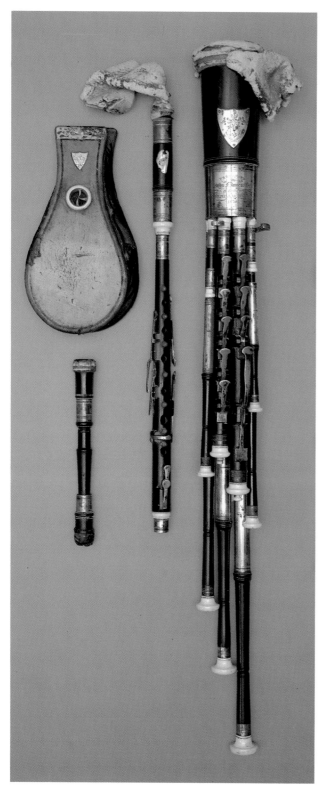

Left

A set of black-wood union pipes with silver and ivory mounts by Robert Reid, North Shields, 1830, stamped on the chanter, stocks and regulators
R. Reid
London £3,960($5,504). 5.IV.84
From the collection of the Millar family

According to an inscription on the drone-stock mount, these pipes were *Presented by Lewis F. Innes, Esqr: of Ballogie to Mr R. Millar, Musician, 1830*. They were sold with a manuscript book of 381 tunes in the hand of Robert Millar, dated *1830*.

Opposite, left

A Venetian guitar inlaid with ivory and mother-of-pearl, school of Matteo Sellas, mid-seventeenth century, repaired by Johann Stoss, Prague, 1829, length of back $18\frac{3}{8}$in (46.6cm)
London £5,500($7,645). 5.IV.84

Opposite, right

A guitar, the back and ribs by Giovanni Hanggele, Milan, 1639, the rest French, mid-nineteenth century, inscribed *ui Hangg * l * in Millano 1639* and labelled *Gio. Hanggele in Milano 1638*, length of back $18\frac{7}{16}$in (46.8cm)
London £8,140($11,315). 21.VI.84

The seventeenth-century part of this instrument is veneered with engraved ivory and kingwood. The central strips on the ribs are engraved with hunting scenes after Hans Bol.

Furniture and tapestries

A pair of George III mahogany armchairs, *circa* 1765
New York $55,000 (£39,568). 29.X.83

A Chinese export black lacquer bureau bookcase with gilt decoration, *circa* 1760,
height 8ft 1½in (247.7cm)
New York $55,000 (£39,568). 29.X.83

One of a pair of George II mahogany armchairs, *circa* 1745
London £121,000 ($168,190). 18.XI.83
From the collection of Miss Elizabeth Humphreys-Owen

This chair was part of a suite of twenty-five chairs and four sofas supplied to the 4th Earl of Shaftesbury for his house, St Giles's, in Dorset.

The D'Arcy cabinet, a George III
mahogany secretaire cabinet
attributed to William Vile, *circa* 1765,
height 6ft $\frac{1}{2}$in (184.2cm)
London £203,500 ($282,865). 18.XI.83

This cabinet was owned by Robert
D'Arcy, 4th Earl of Holderness,
Secretary of State to George III.
Lady Holderness left it in her will to
her granddaughter, Augusta Byron,
half-sister of the poet.

One of a pair of Spanish tortoiseshell and ebony cabinets-on-stands, set with panels of painted glass depicting biblical scenes, mid-seventeenth century, width 6ft 5½in (197cm)
London £41,800 ($58,102). 18.V.84

A maiolica secretaire attributed to the Folco factory, Savona, mid-eighteenth century,
width 4ft 4in (132cm)
Florence L119,780,000 (£51,188 : $70,876). 11.V.84

According to tradition, this secretaire was made by the Folco factory for the villa Gavotti di Albisola,
in which case it is the only surviving piece from the Savona workshop.

The collection of Monsieur Hubert de Saint-Senoch

View of the Pavillon de Bidaine

Monsieur Hubert de Saint-Senoch inherited the basis of the collection from his maternal grandmother, Madame Douine. The family fortune had been made in Les Grands Magasins du Louvre and the collection that she assembled in Paris was housed on the Rue de Varenne. Madame Douine's preference for fine French eighteenth and nineteenth-century furniture, works of art and paintings perfectly expressed the taste of the great collectors in the early decades of the twentieth century. Monsieur de Saint-Senoch, who was himself a collector and patron of the arts, moved the collection to the Pavillon de Bidaine, near Aix-en-Provence (see above).

The emphasis was mainly on architectural pieces of the Régence period with simple marquetry, like the pair of bookcases (see opposite); or refined works of the Louis XVI period, like the consoles (see p. 247). Most of them were unsigned, showing more concern for the intrinsic quality of the pieces, than interest in a particular signature.

The sale of 840 lots took place in Monte Carlo on 4–6 December 1983 and made in total FF28,378,260 (£2,442,191:$3,382,391). Monsieur de Saint-Senoch's library was sold in 246 lots on 7 March 1984 and made in total FF493,950 (£42,509:$58,874).

One of a pair of Régence gilt-bronze-mounted kingwood parquetry bookcases, height 5ft 3¾in (162cm)
Monte Carlo FF2,189,000 (£188,382:$260,906). 4.XII.83
From the collection of the late Monsieur Hubert de Saint-Senoch

One of a pair of Louis XVI satinwood and amaranth consoles, set with a Sèvres blue and white plaque, width 4ft 9½in (146cm)
Monte Carlo FF1,776,000 (£152,840: $211,681). 4.XII.83
From the collection of the late Monsieur Hubert de Saint-Senoch

Opposite
Two from a set of four Louis XIV tapestry hangings, with decoration after Claude Audran III or Jean Bérain, Beauvais or Savonnerie, *circa* 1710, length 10ft 4in (315cm)
Monte Carlo FF888,000 (£76,420: $105,840). 4.XII.83
From the collection of the late Monsieur Hubert de Saint-Senoch

A Régence gilt-bronze-mounted serpentine-front kingwood parquetry commode, stamped *E. Doi,*
width 5ft 3in (160cm)
Monte Carlo FF1,221,000 (£105,077: $145,530), 24.VI.84

This one of the few stamped works by Etienne Doirat.

A Louis XV gilt-bronze-mounted *bois satiné* marquetry bureau plat attributed to Jean-Pierre Latz, width 4ft 11¾in (152cm)
Monte Carlo FF4,662,000(£401,205:$555,662). 25.VI.84

The collection of Florence J. Gould

Born in San Francisco of French parents, the late Florence J. Gould was as much a Frenchwoman as an American: when she died in 1983, at the age of eighty-seven, she bequeathed her fortune to a foundation for the relief of poverty and the promotion of Franco-American friendship. The contents of her villa El Patio, overlooking the sea at Cannes, were sold in Monte Carlo between 24 and 28 June 1984.

Florence Gould belonged to the generation of American women in Paris whose ranks included Gertrude Stein, Picasso's great patron, and Sylvia Beach, who brought Joyce and Hemingway the recognition that they deserved in France. Mrs Gould was renowned as a patron of the arts. In a style reminiscent of the great Parisian salons of the past, she held court first in Paris and later at Cannes. Her guest list from those years reads like a *Who's Who* of French literary and artistic life: Léautaud, Gide, Matisse, Cocteau, Mauriac and Marie Laurençin were among the many to whom she offered friendship and patronage. The prizes she founded, the Max Jacob Poetry Award, the Roger Nimier Prize, the Critics' Award and others, became highlights of the artistic season in Paris. In return, she was named a corresponding member of the Académie des Beaux-Arts and was awarded the Légion d'Honneur.

Around her at El Patio, she assembled paintings and works of art of the highest quality, a fitting setting for her entertaining. The French furniture, lavish silver (see p. 272) and extensive Sèvres dinner service were in regular use. Among a wide range of European eighteenth-century decorations and clocks, a rhinoceros clock with bronzes by Saint-Germain was perhaps the rarest (see p. 252); there was also much Chinese export porcelain (see p. 382) and a fine wood sculpture of Guanyin (see p. 385). Medieval works of art had been her first love (see p. 9) and, as a great bibliophile, she had a fine library (see p. 179).

In total, the sale of 2,223 lots realized FF56,154,700 (£4,832,590: $6,693,051).

One of four Régence gilt-wood armchairs, upholstered in Gobelins tapestry with scenes from
La Fontaine's *Fables*
Monte Carlo FF1,443,000 (£124,182: $171,990). 25.VI.84
From the collection of the late Florence J. Gould

Opposite
A Louis XV gilt-bronze-mounted chiming rhinoceros clock, the base veneered with green horn, the bronzework signed *Saint-Germain*, the clock signed *Gille L'Aîné à Paris*, height 36¼in (92cm)
Monte Carlo FF1,110,000(£95,525:$132,300). 25.VI.84
From the collection of the late Florence J. Gould

Saint-Germain manufactured more than one type of rhinoceros clock. In this example the rhinoceros is perhaps modelled upon the live animal displayed in Paris at the St-Germain fair of 1749; or upon the engravings of it published by Johann Elias Ridinger of Augsburg in 1748–49. Pierre Gille L'Aîné was received Master in 1746; another rhinoceros clock to which he contributed, with an animal by Kaendler, is illustrated on p. 293.

Right
A Louis XV gilt-bronze-mounted double-dialled mantel clock supported by bronze putti, the clock inscribed *Causard, Hger du roi à Paris*, the bronze group attributed to Edmé Bouchardon, height 30in (76cm)
Monte Carlo FF710,400(£61,136:$84,672). 4.XII.83

A gilt-bronze-mounted *bois satiné*, tulipwood and purplewood marquetry commode, stamped
P.A. Foullet, third quarter eighteenth century, width 4ft 9½in (146cm)
New York $159,500(£114,748). 4.V.84
From the collection of Mrs Enid A. Haupt

Pierre-Antoine Foullet was received Master in 1765.

A Louis XV gilt-bronze-mounted black and red lacquer commode, stamped *D.F.*, the mounts marked
with crowned *C*, mid-eighteenth century, width 4ft 4in (132cm)
New York $385,000 (£276,978). 15.X.83

Jean Desforges was received Master in 1739.

The collection of
Mrs Charles Wrightsman

One of a pair of Louis XV gilt-bronze
chenets, attributed to Charles Cressent,
second quarter eighteenth century,
height 1ft 2½in (36.9cm)
New York $132,000 (£94,964). 5.V.84
From the collection of Mrs Charles
Wrightsman

Furniture, works of art and paintings from the collection of Mrs Charles Wrightsman
were offered for sale in New York on 5 May 1984. The Wrightsmans established
themselves as the greatest American collectors of eighteenth-century French art during
the three decades after the Second World War. It is largely as a result of their generosity
that the Metropolitan Museum of Art in New York can boast the best collection of
French eighteenth-century decorative arts in North America; their gift includes whole
rooms, as well as some of the finest surviving pieces of the period.

Early in 1984, Mrs Wrightsman decided to sell her Palm Beach residence and this
housed the part of the collection that was auctioned last May. The furniture included
a Louis XV small bureau plat stamped by Pierre Garnier (see p. 258), a pair of Louis XV
gilt-bronze chenets attributed to Charles Cressent (see above) and a pair of Louis XV
commodes en console, attributed to Jacques Dubois (see opposite). These are believed
to have been made for the Dauphin. It is known that such a pair of consoles was
delivered to the prince in February 1757. Their description in the *Journal* of Lazare
Duvaux corresponds exactly to that of the pair in the Wrightsman Collection. Since
cabinetmakers undertaking commissions for the crown were not required to stamp
their work, the absence of a signature on these pieces reinforces the probability of a
royal provenance.

The sale of 247 lots totalled $4,867,605 (£3,501,874).

One of a pair of Louis XV gilt-bronze-mounted kingwood parquetry commodes en console, attributed to Jacques Dubois, mid-eighteenth century, width 3ft 8¾in (113.8cm)
New York $352,000(£253,237). 5.V.84
From the collection of Mrs Charles Wrightsman

Jacques Dubois was received Master in 1742.

A Louis XV gilt-bronze-mounted purplewood and *bois satiné* parquetry bureau plat, stamped
P. Garnier, JME, mid-eighteenth century, width 4ft 6½in (138.5cm)
New York $269,500(£193,885). 5.V.84
From the collection of Mrs Charles Wrightsman

Pierre Garnier was received Master in 1742.

Opposite
One of a pair of Louis XVI gilt-wood chairs by Georges Jacob
Monte Carlo FF999,000(£85,972:$119,070). 25.VI.84

Georges Jacob was received Master in 1765. These chairs were originally commissioned by the
crown for the *Salon des jeux du roi* in the royal palace at St-Cloud; they were part of an extensive
order placed with Jacob on 31 October 1787.

One of a pair of Louis XVI gilt-wood consoles, last quarter eighteenth century, width 3ft 3¼in (99.7cm)
New York $473,000 (£340,288). 4.V.84

The consoles are after a design by Richard de Lalonde, now in the Kunstbibliothek, Berlin (FRG).
Lalonde was one of the most talented ornamental designers of the period and often executed projects
for the royal residences.

A Federal satinwood and mahogany card table, the carving attributed to Samuel McIntire, Salem,
Massachusetts, *circa* 1798, width 4ft ¾in (123.9cm)
New York $308,000 (£221,583). 28.I.84

Master craftsmen of Newport

Michael Moses

The fame of the Townsend and Goddard cabinet-making families of eighteenth-century Newport has been growing ever since the first issues of *The Magazine Antiques* illustrated several of their documented pieces in the early 1920s. Scholars and collectors have come to recognize that these families made an unequalled contribution to the development of the decorative arts in America. This began with the extensive articles of Cornelius[1] and Isham[2] in the late 1920s and early 1930s; it continued with Downs[3] and Winchester[4] in the 1940s; with Carpenter[5] and Ott[6] in the 1950s and 1960s; and most recently with Heckscher[7] and Moses.[8]

Their particular contribution lies in the integration of architectural and decorative elements to develop unique variations on standard forms. Their crowning achievement is the so-called 'block-and-shell' furniture, which reached its artistic zenith in the nine six-shell and one nine-shell secretaires that are known to survive (Fig. 2). While the secretaire was a common form in both Europe and America during the eighteenth century, no other group of makers integrated the bonnet top (an American contribution) with the bookcase section by using applied and raised scroll-board panels; or carried the three-panel blocking of the desk section up through the desk lid and cabinet doors; or capped the blocking with wavy lobed shells. This integration of architectural elements (vertical blocking) and decorative elements (shell carving) is also exemplified in their great block-and-shell kneehole desks (Fig. 1) and bureaus.

The creative energies of the two families were not confined to case furniture. Their contribution to cabriole-leg furniture was also substantial. In their highboys (Fig. 3), they combined the bonnet top with the upper case of drawers by repeating raised panels in the scroll board. They integrated the lower case shell into the apron, rather than the lower central drawer, which was the normal approach in Boston and Philadelphia. The use of webless open-talon claw feet was never better executed than on Townsend and Goddard cabriole-leg furniture (Figs 3–4). The integration of cyma-shaped curves in both the horizontal and vertical plane was also achieved with great success.

Fortunately, enough documented furniture has survived to allow us to develop a method of attributing undocumented works to individual members of this family, based on calligraphy, ornament and construction. John Townsend used a unique method of construction for all of his eighteen documented tables, making it possible

Fig. 1
A Chippendale shell-carved and block-front mahogany kneehole dressing table, Goddard-Townsend school, Newport, Rhode Island, *circa* 1760, width 2ft 11½in (90.2cm)
New York $385,000 (£276,978). 22.X.83

This dressing table originally belonged to William Ellery of Newport, Rhode Island, who signed the Declaration of Independence.

to assign a maker to any table with the same technique. Other elements of design and construction indicate that the highboy in Fig. 3 can also be attributed to him.

There are fewer documented pieces by other members of these families, so it is less easy to establish the same level of authentification for their work. However, the pair of chairs illustrated in Fig. 4 have claw-and-ball feet and a shell in their crest rail so similar to those on documented pieces that they must be by a member of John Goddard's family. Several kneehole desks and bureaus have shell design and construction techniques that allow their attribution to Edmund Townsend. Our ability to assign undocumented works to particular makers will continue to improve as more documented examples come to light.

Fig. 2
A nine-shell mahogany secretaire, Goddard-Townsend
school, *circa* 1750–70, height 8ft 9in (266.7cm)
Reproduced courtesy of the Rhode Island
Historical Society

Fig. 3
A mahogany highboy by John Townsend,
circa 1760–75, height 6ft 10¾in (210.2cm)
Reproduced courtesy of Bernard & S. Dean Levy,
Inc., New York City

Fig. 4
A pair of Chippendale mahogany side chairs, Goddard-Townsend school, Newport, Rhode Island, *circa* 1765
New York $143,000 (£102,878). 28.I.84

A similar chair in the Metropolitan Museum of Art, New York, is probably from the same set.

NOTES
1. C. Cornelius, 'John Townsend, An Eighteenth-Century Cabinetmaker', *Metropolitan Museum Studies I*, 1928, pp. 72–80
2. N. Isham, 'John Goddard and his Work', *Bulletin, Rhode Island School of Design*, vol. 15, April 1927
3. J. Downs, 'The Furniture of Goddard and Townsend', *The Magazine Antiques*, 52, 1947, pp. 427–31
4. A. Winchester, 'The Goddard and Townsend Joiners, Part I', *The Magazine Antiques*, 49, 1946, pp. 228–31; 'Part II', 49, 1946, pp. 292–95
5. R. E. Carpenter, Jr, *The Arts and Crafts of Newport, Rhode Island, 1640–1820* (1954)
6. J. K. Ott, *Rhode Island Furniture 1730–1810* (1965)
7. M. H. Heckscher, 'John Townsend's Block and Shell Furniture', *The Magazine Antiques*, May 1982, pp. 1144–52
8. L. and M. Moses, 'Authenticating John Townsend's and John Goddard's Queen Anne and Chippendale Tables', *The Magazine Antiques*, May 1982, pp. 1130–43; M. Moses, *Master Craftsmen of Newport: The Townsend and Goddard Families* (1984)

A rosewood and tulipwood display cabinet with painted decoration, from a nine-piece dining-room suite designed by W. H. Windrige, *circa* 1890, height 7ft 11in (241.5cm)
London £11,000 ($15,290). 17.II.84

One of a set of six gilt-bronze-mounted boulle salon chairs, possibly English, *circa* 1840
London £10,120 ($14,067). 11.XI.83

A Flemish *feuilles de chou* tapestry, Enghien, mid-sixteenth century,
10ft 8in by 14ft 2in (325cm by 432cm)
New York $93,500(£67,266). 3.III.84

Opposite
A Louis XV Gobelins tapestry, *Novembre, les semailles; signe du Sagittaire*, by Pierre-François
Cozette, signed and dated *1770*, 13ft 1in by 9ft 5in (398cm by 287cm)
Monte Carlo FF666,000(£57,315: $79,380). 4.XII.83

This was one of a pair of tapestries presented by Louis XV to the Archbishop of Turin, grand almoner
to the King of Sardinia, on the occasion of the marriage of the Comte d'Artois to Marie-Thérèse of
Savoy in October 1773.

Silver

A Mary Tudor silver-gilt casting bottle, London, 1553, height $5\frac{7}{8}$in (14.8cm)
London £110,000 ($152,900). 3.V.84

This is among the rarest pieces of Tudor plate, one of only three fully marked flacons in the form of a pilgrim bottle to survive from the sixteenth century. These small bottles contained rosewater, or some other scent, for sprinkling over the hands after a meal.

Eight freedom boxes and a pair of ceremonial thimbles from a group of eighteen freedom boxes and seven associated items presented to members of the FitzGerald family, *circa* 1710–1838
London, total £224,895 ($312,604). 3.V.84
From the collection of the Duke of Leinster

Two George II cake baskets, bearing the arms of Townshend quartering Lee and Glegg for Lee Porcher Townshend, maker's mark of Paul de Lamerie, London, 1737 and 1740, diameter $14\frac{1}{2}$in (37cm) Monte Carlo FF2,331,000 (£200,602: $277,831). 26.VI.84
From the collection of the late Florence J. Gould

A pair of George IV silver-gilt double wine-coaster wagons, bearing the arms of Drax quartering Erle, Sawbridge and others, makers' mark of E., E., J. & W. Barnard for Edward Barnard & Sons, London, 1829, stamped *D. Ellis London Fecit*, length 19⅞in (50.5cm)
London £121,000 ($168,190). 3.V.84

Little is known about David Ellis, retail jeweller and silversmith of Oxford Street, London. During his twenty-five years or so of trading, Ellis stocked a number of exceptional pieces of plate, of which these are without doubt the most sumptuous. According to the entry in Edward Barnard & Sons' Day Book, they were supplied to Ellis at a cost of £187 19s 10d.

Opposite
Left and right A pair of George II ewers, bearing the royal arms, maker's mark of John Hugh Le Sage, London, 1748, height 16⅞in (43cm)
London £60,500 ($84,095). 3.V.84
Centre A George II christening bowl and cover, bearing the royal arms, inscribed *Lady Emilia Lenos Oct 25th 1731*, maker's mark of Edward Feline, London, *circa* 1730, width 14¾in (37.5cm)
London £77,000 ($107,030). 3.V.84

These three pieces from the collection of the Duke of Leinster are almost certainly christening gifts from George II to his godchildren: the ewers for George FitzGerald, Lord Offaly; the bowl for Lady Emelia Lenox, christened at St Margaret's, Westminster, 31 October 1731.

The Shield of Achilles
by John Flaxman, RA

Shirley Bury and Michael Snodin

The silver-gilt Shield of Achilles (Fig. 1), designed and modelled by one of the greatest English sculptors of the Regency, is an outstanding instance of a synthesis of the fine and decorative arts.[1] The designer, John Flaxman, was the most illustrious of the Royal Academicians associated with Rundell, Bridge & Rundell of Ludgate Hill in the City of London. The firm were the Royal Goldsmiths to George III and his family.

Flaxman's inspiration was the shield made by Hephaestus for Achilles, described by Homer in the eighteenth book of the *Iliad*. A considerable interval elapsed between the inception and realization of the shield. Flaxman first essayed it in his book-illustration *Thetis bringing the armour to Achilles*, engraved for him by Thomas Piroli in 1793 (Fig. 2). The shield held by Thetis is depicted with the sun in the centre and figures sketchily indicated in the wide border, which is edged with a wave pattern, the one constant element in the artist's various later treatments of the theme. His final version was produced in an edition of four silver-gilt examples, together with others in bronze and a number of plaster casts. The silver-gilt shields went respectively to George IV, in time to form part of a traditional buffet display at his coronation banquet in July 1821, the Duke of York, the Earl of Lonsdale[2] and the Duke of Northumberland.

In creating his shield, Flaxman had access to reference material at Rundell's, including a cast of the largest of three basins in the early seventeenth-century Lomellini service (Fig. 3).[3] The complete service comprised three pairs of ewers and basins; the largest pair were acquired by the Victoria & Albert Museum in 1974; the other two went to the Ashmolean and Fitzwilliam Museums. All six items bear the arms of the Lomellini family.[4] The service was at the Royal Goldsmiths in 1807, possibly for cleaning or repair. The poet and gossip Samuel Rogers saw it in the shop and mentioned it in a letter to Lady Dunmore, dated 8 November. 'The plate Lord S.[haftesbury][5] bought at Naples for £300', he wrote, 'is the handsomest I ever saw – three vast dishes and three ewers richly sculptured like the Shield of Achilles, with battles, processions, etc.'[6] Despite Rogers's reference to a 'Shield of Achilles', it is doubtful whether the sculptor had yet embarked on his grand design in 1807. He was probably referring to Homer's description, which was familiar to everyone with a conventional classical education or access, for instance, to Pope's translation of the work.

Artists before Flaxman had tried to give Homer's shield visual expression, but failed by being literalistic (Fig. 4). Flaxman on the other hand was selective and even innovative. His central image of Apollo is a substitute for Homer's 'ever-circling sun', which earlier artists had placed in the inner border. Even in his book-illustration (Fig. 2), the artist shows the boss in the middle dominated by the sun.

Fig. 1
A silver-gilt cast of the Shield of Achilles, designed and modelled by John Flaxman, maker's mark of
Philip Rundell for Rundell, Bridge & Rundell, London, 1822–23, diameter 36¼in (92cm)
London £484,000 ($672,760). 3.V.84
From the collection of the Duke of Northumberland, KG, GCVO, TD, PC

There are two pairs of rings on the back, to which leather thongs would have been attached so that the
heavy shield could be carried. The back is also engraved with the badge of Hugh, 3rd Duke of
Northumberland (1785–1847), who acquired the shield from Rundells, and inscribed *DESIGNED &
MODELLED BY JOHN FLAXMAN.RA EXECUTED & PUBLISHED BY RUNDELL, BRIDGE &
RUNDELL. GOLDSMITHS & JEWELLERS. TO HIS MAJESTY, LONDON MDCCCXXII.*

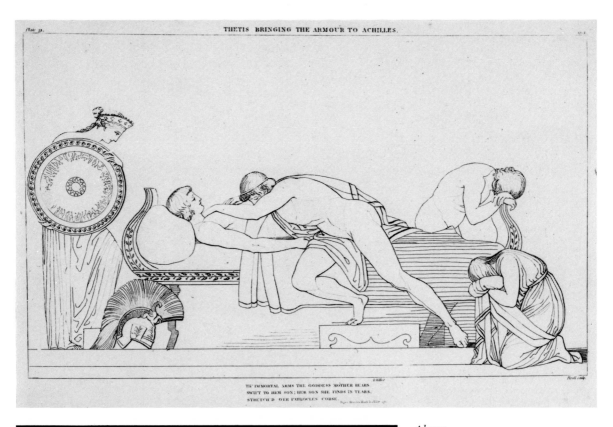

THETIS BRINGING THE ARMOUR TO ACHILLES.

TH' IMMORTAL ARMS THE GODDESS MOTHER BEARS
SWIFT TO HER SON; HER SON SHE FINDS IN TEARS,
STRETCH'D O'ER PATROCLUS CORSE.

Above
Fig. 2
Thetis bringing the armour to Achilles, an engraving after Flaxman by Thomas Piroli, from the *Iliad* (1793), pl. 31

Fig. 3
A silver basin, bearing the arms of the Lomellini family, maker's mark *GA* over *B* within a trefoil, probably for G. A. Belga, Genoa, 1621–22, diameter 25¼in (64.1cm)
Reproduced courtesy of the Trustees of the Victoria & Albert Museum, London

Fig. 4
A design for a Shield of Achilles by Simon
Gribelin II, after Nicolas Vleughels, from Jean
Boivin's *Apologie d'Homère et Bouclier d'Achille*
(1715)

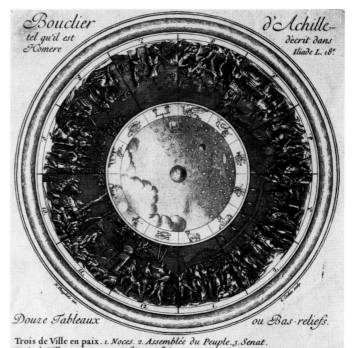

Below
Fig. 5
The Pleiades, an engraving by William Blake,
circa 1816, after a Flaxman drawing of 1807,
from Hesiod's *Theogony* (1817), pl. 18

The poet's celestial theme, as finally interpreted by Flaxman, is expressed by Apollo emerging from a background of rays and driving his chariot over a full moon. The god is surrounded by the constellations and the whole is enclosed by a border of stars. The graceful figures of the Pleiades flanking Apollo derive from Flaxman's book-illustration (Fig. 5). The broad outer border, with the 'mighty stream of ocean' on the rim, is filled with figure groups following the order of Homer's terrestrial concerns. Beginning at the bottom right and proceeding anti-clockwise are a marriage procession, a banquet and dancing; a siege, ambuscade and military engagement; a harvest field; a vintage scene; and shepherds defending their herds against an attack by lions.

The first recorded design forms the principal subject of a fulsome letter from the Royal Goldsmiths to the artist, dated 29 October 1810. Two payments were enclosed, including one for a hundred guineas for the 'beautiful design of the Shield of Achilles', in token of the firm's admiration.[7] On other evidence, the 'design' seems to have consisted of four models and six drawings.[8] The respectful, even adulatory, tone of the letter emphasizes the privileged status of Flaxman and his fellow artists at Rundell's. According to the anonymous author of the *Memoirs of the late Philip Rundell, Esq.*, which appeared shortly after the latter's death in 1827, Flaxman, furnished with an edition of the *Iliad* 'nearly as tall as himself' (the artist was very short, with a deformed back), read aloud long extracts to the partners and then discoursed upon them.[9] If Flaxman's sister-in-law Maria Denman was correct in asserting that he worked from the original Greek text and not from a translation, as Cunningham stated in his *Lives* of 1833,[10] Philip Rundell's self-control on these occasions was commendable. Known to his staff as 'Vinegar', in contrast to 'Oil' (his principal partner, John Bridge), Rundell had 'never professed himself a scholar'. He was apparently glad to relinquish to his better-educated nephews Edmond Waller Rundell and Thomas Bigge, and to 'Mr Bridge',[11] who was 'conversant with the best authors, the earlier stages of the production under review, which was finally accomplished at the private manufactory of the firm in Dean-street Soho'.[12]

The account in the *Memoirs* of Flaxman's exposition of the Homeric theme suggests an overriding enthusiasm on the part of the artist, which probably had to find immediate expression in drawings and models. The readings may therefore have taken place earlier in 1810. The firm's letter of 29 October envisaged that the design would be executed under Flaxman's 'occasional inspection' by 'Mr Theed'. This was the sculptor William Theed the Elder, a junior director of the Royal Goldsmiths, who died in 1817, by which time Flaxman himself was at work on the final model.

More than ten drawings for the shield survive,[13] from which it is possible to predicate two main stages in Flaxman's design. The earlier stage, known in its complete form in a drawing after Flaxman,[14] has the central disc encircled by clumsily composed signs of the Zodiac, which follow Homer's description more literally than the later version. Earlier interpreters had framed the scenes in the broad border separately, probably to represent the five parts of Hephaestus's shield.[15] While dispensing even in the first stage with clear divisions in his border, Flaxman nevertheless indicated the different subjects by spaces or architectural features. Among the latter is a door, representing doors mentioned in the *Iliad*, which can be seen on the left of the design in Fig. 6; it is clear from the corresponding detail in the shield (Fig. 7) that it was later

Fig. 6
JOHN FLAXMAN, RA
Design for the marriage procession
Pen and ink and wash, first version, *circa* 1810, 7½in by 14in (19.1cm by 35.5cm)
Reproduced courtesy of the Trustees of the British Museum, London

Fig. 7
Detail of the marriage procession from Flaxman's Shield of Achilles

omitted. No second-stage drawing for the procession survives; it was presumably destroyed in the working of the model. The artist's other preparatory sketches of the first and second stages show that in every case the border was originally conceived as a straight frieze. The unsatisfactory slackness of the first design, which probably became apparent when the border was adapted to the curve, was no doubt one of the reasons for its revision.

External considerations seem also to have prompted Flaxman's revised design. The growing list of Wellington's successes in the Peninsula had invested the project with a patriotic significance from the first. The author of the *Memoirs* held that the shield was conceived in tribute to the future Duke, the cost of the design and manufacture being partly defrayed by 'the munificence of several spirited individuals, by each of whom a cast was ordered'.[16] A sketch portrays the shield as a military trophy (Fig. 8).[17]

In 1814, however, the shield still unrealized, Flaxman's old friend, the painter Thomas Stothard, won a competition for the design of another silver shield to be presented to the Duke by the merchants and bankers of London (Fig. 9). Stothard was one of Rundell's artists; his Bacchus and Ariadne sideboard dishes (Fig. 10), hallmarked

Opposite
Fig. 8
JOHN FLAXMAN, RA
Study for the Shield of Achilles as part of a trophy
Pen and ink and wash,
6⅞in by 7⅞in (17.3cm by 20cm)
Reproduced courtesy of the Trustees of the British Museum, London

Fig. 9
The Wellington Shield, designed by
Thomas Stothard, maker's mark of
Benjamin Smith, Senior and Junior, for
Green, Ward & Green, London, 1822–23
Reproduced courtesy of the Trustees of
the Victoria & Albert Museum, London
(The Wellington Collection,
Apsley House)

Fig. 10
One of a pair of George III silver-gilt
sideboard dishes, with a central group
of Bacchus and Ariadne, designed by
Thomas Stothard, maker's mark of
Paul Storr, Storr & Co., for Rundell,
Bridge & Rundell, London, 1813–14,
diameter of each 30½in (77.5cm)
London £286,000($397,540). 3.V.84
From the collection of the Duke of
Northumberland, KG, GCVO, TD, PC

for 1813 onwards, were executed in the firm's Dean Street workshops, then directed by Paul Storr.[18] Nevertheless, the commission for the manufacture of Stothard's Wellington Shield went not to Rundell's, as might have been expected, but to their rivals Green, Ward & Green. They drove home their triumph by sub-contracting the work to Benjamin Smith, who had once been in charge of Rundell's first workshop at Lime Kiln Lane, Greenwich.[19] It must have been small comfort to the Royal Goldsmiths that Stothard's design was not finally executed in silver until about 1822. They were saddled meanwhile with an expensive commitment that had lost its novelty. The only way to fight back was to ensure that Flaxman's shield surpassed Stothard's.

Flaxman referred to 'the fragments of the shield in progress' in a letter of 15 May 1814 to William Sotheby,[20] which does not suggest a major reworking. But writing to his friend and patron, the poet William Hayley, on 8 September following, Flaxman wryly lamented that 'Achilles teazes me for his Sheild [sic]'. His wife Nancy added in a postscript that 'he has at the desire of Mess.rs Rundle recommenc'd the Model of the famous Shield upon a larger Plan –',[21] though whether in terms of size or content is not made clear. Flaxman's changes were completed by 1817, and the figure groups combined into a continuous rhythmical sequence of remarkable subtlety. On 4 January 1817 he noted in his account book the receipt of £200 'on account of the Sheild of Achilles', followed on 20 January 1818 by £525, for what was presumably the final model, on which he had himself worked and from which the casting moulds were made.[22] Thus he received at least £825 in all for the various drawings and models.

The profits to Rundell's cannot have been large. They had to pay for the silver, at a cost later computed by the historical painter George Foggo as up to £250 for each of the four silver-gilt shields, as well as the materials for the bronze versions.[23] The services of the casters and chasers also had to be paid for, although Flaxman, working from his own drawings, finished his final plaster model with meticulous care in order to minimize the chasing of the casts.[24] The first silver cast came up to his expectations. 'I have seen the cast in Silver for the Sheild', he wrote to Thomas Bigge in late September 1819, 'which is indeed very successful &, [sic] perfect so that little finishing seems needful to the faces of Minerva or Mars [Pallas Athena and Ares] or to the other more delicate parts of the Basso relievo & consequently the less the Chaser has to do the more the metal will resemble the model'.[25] The silver-gilt shields were the culmination of the design. The first casts had been made in bronze and Foggo held that they had been worked on by William Pitts the Younger, a sculptor who was also one of the most celebrated chasers of his day, much used by Rundell's.[26] Pitts may have assisted with the silver versions before they were gilt, but they remain more nearly Flaxman's autography than any other work of his for the Royal Goldsmiths.

NOTES

1. Sotheby's, *Catalogue of Important Silver and Gold*, London, 3 May 1984, lot 124, from the collection of the Duke of Northumberland

2. George IV's shield remains in the Royal Collection; the Duke of York's, after passing through various hands, came into the possession of the Huntington Collection, San Marino, California, in 1973;

the Earl of Lonsdale's was sold in 1947 and is now in Anglesey Abbey, Cambridgeshire (National Trust). See John Culme's commentary in the Sotheby catalogue, op. cit., pp. 82–83

3. A cast of a 'shield' representing the 'reception of the Doria' was sold from the Bridge Collection in 1911 (Waring & Gillow Ltd, *Catalogue . . . of the Highly Interesting and Valuable Collection of Works of Art . . . formed by J. Bridge & J. Gawler Bridge*, The Manor House, Piddletrenthide, 20–22 September 1911, lot 393). John Bridge had been a partner at Rundell's. A bearded recumbent figure in the centre of the smaller Lomellini basins recalls Bronzino's portrait of Andrea Doria as Neptune (see H. MacAndrew, 'Genoese Silver on loan to the Ashmolean Museum', *The Burlington Magazine*, CIV, 1972, pp. 611–20), while the largest basin bears scenes celebrating a Grimaldi general. As both the Grimaldi and the Doria were Genoese families, perhaps it was mistakenly assumed that the latter scenes celebrated the Doria, in which case the cast in the Bridge sale may have been taken from the largest Lomellini basin.

4. H. MacAndrew, op. cit.

5. Presumably Anthony Ashley Cooper, 5th Earl of Shaftesbury (1761–1811), and not his grandfather, the 3rd Earl, who resided in Naples between 1711 and his death in 1712/13.

6. H. Maxwell, *The Honourable Charles Murray, KCB: a Memoir* (1898), p. 11

7. The letter of 29 October 1810, signed by Rundell, Bridge & Rundell, is mounted on f. 98 of a blue vellum album of Flaxman letters given by C. F. Murray to the Fitzwilliam Museum in 1909 (Department of Manuscripts).

8. See Sotheby catalogue, op. cit., p. 84; the information was discovered by John Culme in an exchange of letters between Maria Denman, Flaxman's sister-in-law, and Rundell, Bridge & Co., 1843 (British Museum, Add. MS 39791, ff. 63/64,90, 282/3).

9. *Memoirs of the late Philip Rundell, Esq., by a gentleman for many years connected with the firm* (1827), pp. 21–23

10. See Sotheby catalogue, op. cit., p. 78

11. 'Mr. Bridge' was either John Bridge or his nephew, John Gawler Bridge, who was of the same generation as E. W. Rundell and Thomas Bigge.

12. See n. 9

13. The drawings are in the British Museum, the Victoria & Albert Museum, the Huntington Collection, the Paul Oppé Collection and (ex) Christopher Powney Collection.

14. This drawing, in pen and ink and wash (private collection), is the only record of the first version of the centre, although the early border is also shown in a drawing in the Victoria & Albert Museum. Most of the drawings in the British Museum are sketches for the first stage.

15. See Fig. 4. An Achilles shield, curiously similar to Flaxman's, both in its scenes and sun chariot ringed by stars, is illustrated in Quatremère de Quincy, *Le Jupiter Olympien* (1814). Quatremère was in England before 1815 to see the Elgin Marbles and perhaps met Flaxman. The scenes in his border are, however, in two ranges and strictly separated.

16. See Sotheby catalogue, op. cit.; see also n. 9

17. Another drawing in the British Museum shows the shield in the centre of an elaborate sideboard display (Print Room, Flaxman Royal IV, Box 71; 1900–8–24–198).

18. See Sotheby catalogue, op. cit., p. 68, lot 105, for a pair of these sideboard dishes. An example in the Royal Collection, hallmarked for 1814–15, is illustrated in David Irwin, *John Flaxman 1755–1826* (1979), p. 198.

19. S. Bury, 'The Lengthening Shadow of Rundell's', *Connoisseur*, CLXI, 1966, p. 81

20. See Sotheby catalogue, op. cit., p. 81. The letter is in the Huntington Collection.

21. See n. 7; f. 47

22. Flaxman Account Book, Columbia University, f. 80

23. *Report from Select Committee on Arts and Manufactures; together with the Minutes of Evidence . . .* (1835), pp. 52–53, paras 691–93

24. According to the sculptor Nollekens, Flaxman cast his model in plaster himself and then sharpened the cast by carving (J. T. Smith, *Nollekens and his Times* (1828), vol. II, p. 446). This cast was included in the Bridge sale of 1911 (see n. 3), lot 300a.

25. Letters from John Flaxman to Thomas Bigge (private collection)

26. William Pitts, the son of a silversmith and chaser associated with Rundell's, trained as a sculptor at the Royal Academy Schools; he committed suicide in 1840, leaving uncompleted his own Shield of Aeneas.

A set of four George III salts, bearing the monogram of Harriet Mellon, Duchess of St Albans, maker's mark of Paul Storr for Rundell, Bridge & Rundell, London, 1813, stamped *Rundell, Bridge et Rundell*, height 4½ in (11.4cm)
New York $198,000 (£142,446). 21.VI.84

The configuration of a shell with a Triton above swirling waves appears in the monumental bronze sculpture of *Thetis returning from Vulcan with arms for Achilles*, in the collection of HM the Queen, by William Theed, RA, of 1812. Theed, initially an associate and later a partner in the firm of Rundell, Bridge & Rundell, was probably the designer of these salts.

A parcel-gilt jewel casket, bearing the royal arms of France, maker's mark of Marc-Augustin Lebrun,
Paris, *circa* 1824, length 23⅛in (58.8cm)
New York $112,200(£80,719). 21.VI.84
From the collection of Mr and Mrs Abran Spanel

The workmanship and subject matter, scenes from the life of Don Quixote, suggest that the panels
were made in Spain. The casket may have been a gift from Spain to Charles X, perhaps for his
coronation, which took place on 29 May 1825.

A silver-gilt sideboard dish, maker's mark *SB*, Genoa, 1621, diameter 23⅝in (60cm)
Monte Carlo FF999,000 (£85,972:$119,070). 6.XII.83

Four goddesses in cartouches are embossed on the outer border, Juno, Diana, Venus and Minerva; on
the inner border, Neptune rescues Amymone from a satyr, while the central roundel depicts the rape
of Europa. This piece can be compared with a dish dated 1619 in the Ashmolean Museum, Oxford,
which illustrates the four loves of Jupiter and the triumph of Neptune.

Opposite
Two silver-gilt tazzas, maker's mark a bird's claw, Delft, 1604 and 1606, diameter 7½in (19cm)
Geneva SFr935,000 (£298,722:$413,717). 15.V.84

The bowls are embossed with emblematic scenes of the seasons and the elements, perhaps influenced
by prints of Johann Sadeler the Elder.

Two silver-gilt figures of stags, maker's mark of Johann Ludwig Biller I, Augsburg, *circa* 1700, height overall 24⅝in (62.5cm)
Geneva SFr605,000 (£193,291:$267,699). 15.V.84

Johann Ludwig Biller was a member of the famous Augsburg family of goldsmiths. They received many royal commissions, but few of their major works survive.

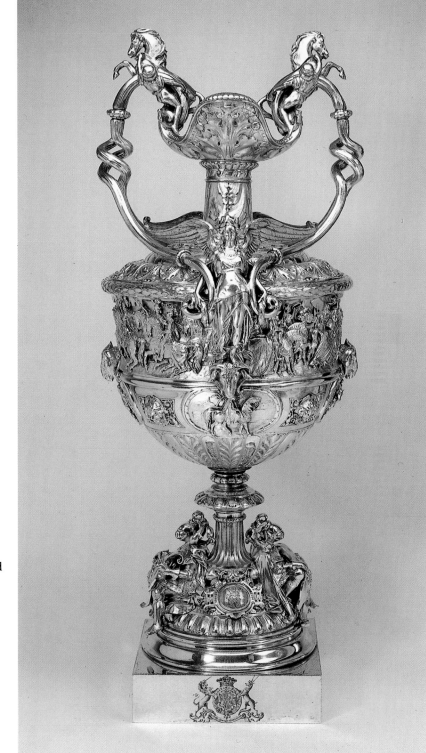

The Orléans Cup, a silver-gilt
presentation vase for the Goodwood
Races, bearing the arms of the
Duc d'Orléans and the Duke of
Richmond, made by M. Durand
from designs and models by
Jean-Baptiste-Jules Klagmann,
Paris, *circa* 1840,
height of vase 26in (66cm)
London £57,200 ($79,508). 9.VII.84

The cup was donated by the Duc
d'Orléans in 1841 and won by the
Duke of Richmond's bay hunter,
Mus. It was later shown at the
Great Exhibition of 1851.

European ceramics
and glass

A Faenza maiolica dish painted by Baldassare Manara, signed on the reverse,
circa 1535, diameter 8½ in (21.5cm)
London £20,900 ($29,051). 22.XI.83
From the collection of P. Damiron, Esq.

A Flörsheim figure of a parrot, marked with *FH* in black, 1780–90, height 13in (33cm)
London £17,600 ($24,464). 22.XI.83

A Meissen group of fighting harlequins from the *commedia dell'arte*, modelled by Johann Joachim Kaendler, marked with crossed swords in underglaze blue, *circa* 1740, height 6¼in (16cm) London £27,500 ($38,225). 12.VI.84

A Meissen group of *The mockery of age*, modelled by Johann Joachim Kaendler, 1741–45, height 7⅜in (18.8cm) New York $42,900 (£30,863). 13.X.83 From the collection of the Metropolitan Museum of Art, New York

This group, which has been known by a variety of titles, including *The invalid duped*, served as the inspiration for later Vienna and Derby models. Kaendler described it in detail in his workbook of 1740–48, when it cost 18 thalers.

A Louis XV gilt-bronze-mounted rhinoceros clock, the Meissen group of a Turk on a rhinoceros modelled by Johann Joachim Kaendler, 1752–55, the clock inscribed *Gille L'Aîné A PARIS*, the clock and mounts, 1760–75, height 21⅞in (55.6cm)
New York $51,700(£37,194). 13.X.83

Early in 1741 an Indian rhinoceros arrived in Europe, the fifth on record. The animal was taken on a Grand Tour and arrived at Dresden in April 1747, where it was seen by Frederick Augustus, Elector of Saxony and King of Poland, and the Meissen sculptor, Kaendler; it was probably Kaendler himself who modelled the two subsequent Meissen figures of the beast, of which this is the second. Another rhinoceros clock with a movement by the same maker is illustrated on p. 252.

A Vincennes watering can, marked with interlaced *L*s in blue, 1753, height $7\frac{7}{8}$ in (20cm)
London £30,800 ($42,812). 12.VI.84

This is one of only five such *arrosoirs* that are known to have survived, another being offered in the
same sale. The fine spray produced by the rose might lend credence to the story that Madame de
Pompadour used porcelain cans to sprinkle her tubs of Vincennes flowers with scent.

A Vincennes tankard and cover, marked with interlaced *L*s in blue, *circa* 1753, height 6in (15.3cm)
London £36,300 ($50,457). 12.VI.84
From the collection of the late Mrs K. Gifford-Scott

This tankard is now in the Nelson-Atkins Museum of Art, Kansas City. A similar one is in the Palazzo Pitti, Florence, and another in the Musée des Arts Décoratifs in Paris.

A Sèvres *rose pompadour* ewer and basin, the basin marked with interlaced *L*s in blue, 1757, height of ewer 7½in (19cm), width of basin 11⅜in (29cm)
London £126,500 ($175,835). 12.VI.84

A *Vincennes ewer and basin*, marked with interlaced *L*s in blue, *circa* 1753, height of ewer 9½in (24.2cm), width of basin 14⅛in (36cm) London £22,000 ($30,580). 12.VI.84

From the collection of the late Mrs K. Gifford-Scott and now in the Victoria & Albert Museum, London

A Sèvres dinner service, marked with interlaced *L*s, 1753–90
Monte Carlo FF1,054,500(£90,749: $125,685). 4.XII.83

From left to right
A Chelsea plate, marked with brown anchor, *circa* 1754–56, diameter 9¾in (24.8cm).
London £2,200 ($3,058). 14.II.84
A Chelsea dish, marked with red anchor, *circa* 1754–56, diameter 14½in (36.9cm).
London £5,720 ($7,951). 14.II.84
A Chelsea plate, marked with red anchor, *circa* 1754–56, diameter 9⅝in (24.5cm).
London £2,530 ($3,517).14.II.84

From left to right
A Chelsea fig box and cover, *circa* 1752–56, height 4in (10.2cm)
London £4,840 ($6,728). 22.V.84
A Chelsea leveret tureen and cover, marked with red anchor on cover, *circa* 1752–56,
length 3¾in (9.5cm)
London £4,620 ($6,422). 22.V.84

'By the peacock!'

Michael R. Turner

'By the peacock!' was at one time a common but sacred oath, sworn to a bird whose fabled incorruptibility of the flesh led to its adoption as an emblem of immortality. Over the years this most exotic member of the pheasant family, *Pavo cristatus*, has been both an object of superstition and veneration: the attribute of the goddess Juno; worshipped by the Hindus. More prosaically, it was suitably dressed by the Romans to form the centrepiece of a feast. In the deranged mind of George III it became a word to be added to the end of each sentence in his parliamentary address. Fortunately he was persuaded that it should be whispered, rather than spoken aloud, and the resultant silences gave a most dramatic effect. John Ruskin in *The Stones of Venice* coupled the peacock with the lily: 'Remember that the most beautiful things in the world are also the most useless; peacocks and lilies for instance.' Suitably, with the lily, it became an unofficial emblem of the Aesthetic Movement.

The peacock's distinctive and brilliant plumage, ideally suited to stylization, has ensured its success as a motif in the ceramic arts. It was modelled by J. J. Kaendler at Meissen in 1734 and other models are recorded in England at Chelsea and Bow in about 1755, followed by Derby and Minton in the nineteenth century. The 'majolica' glazes developed at Minton in about 1850 under their art director, Léon Arnoux, took their inspiration from Italian Renaissance maiolica. The violet-blue, emerald-green and ochre-yellow colours especially suited Mintons' exceptionally large peacock model (see opposite). Its sculptor Paul Comolera (1818–97) specialized in bird subjects and worked at Mintons between 1873 and 1875, earning £17 6s 8d a month.

Of the eight presently recorded Mintons 'majolica' peacocks, one in particular has an unusual history. Now on display at Flagstaff Hill, Port of Warnambool, Victoria, it was originally sent by sea in the iron clipper *Loch Ard* to be exhibited in Melbourne at the 'First Australian International Exhibition' of 1880. Before arrival, the *Loch Ard* was wrecked near The Caves, on the coast of Victoria. The cask containing the bird floated into a narrow gorge and was salvaged by a Mr Miller. After the death of his daughter in 1936, it was purchased by the government of Victoria for $4,500. Another peacock came to roost in the Isle of Wight. It was purchased by Mrs Sadie Woods, owner of the Shanklin Pier, for £2. Today it is much admired by the guests of the aptly named Peacock Vane Hotel, near Ventnor. A third is in the Mintons Museum, Stoke-on-Trent. An albumen print of an unglazed model, shape no. 2045, appears in the factory pattern books preserved in the museum's archives. This presumably means that the model was made to order, although no contemporary price is given. Whilst expensive, it would have cost considerably less than the sum paid at auction last February.

A Mintons 'majolica' peacock, after
a model by Paul Comolera, moulded
signature, *circa* 1875,
height 60in (152.4cm)
London £18,700 ($25,993). 14.II.84

Paul Comolera was born in Paris and
completed his studies at the Rue
d'Enfer as a pupil of François Rude.
He made his début at the Salon of
1846 with a group of *Golden pheasants
of China*. The majority of his works
were cast in bronze, but some of his
models were produced in faïence by
Hautin & Boulanger at Choisy-le-Roi
and others in 'majolica' by Mintons.

The collection of
Mr and Mrs Fritz Biemann

A transparent-enamelled beaker decorated
by Samuel Mohn, signed and dated *1814*,
Dresden, height 3¼in (8.3cm)
London £27,500 ($38,225). 16.VI.84
From the collection of Mr and
Mrs Fritz Biemann

The European glass assembled by Fritz Biemann, a Swiss businessman, and his wife
was comparable in its range and quality to the celebrated Krug Collection, sold recently
by Sotheby's. Since the Second World War, the Biemanns have been among the most
passionate collectors in this field. They decided to sell part of the collection in order
to concentrate on the areas that have come to interest them most; early Venetian and
German enamelled glass.

The sale was held to coincide with the Ceramics Fair at the Dorchester Hotel and
contained pieces from all the important European glass-making centres. A Venetian
bowl in agate glass or 'calcedonio', at £25,300, reflected the rarity of early pieces in
this technique. The collection was particularly strong in Nuremberg glass: a signed
allegorical goblet by Hermann Schwinger and a part-purple coloured goblet and
cover made, respectively, £22,000 and £33,000; the most important piece in the sale
was arguably a beaker decorated by Johann Schaper (see opposite). Among pieces
from the Rhineland were a green-tinted roemer with rare gilt decoration (see p. 304)
and another engraved by a Dutch master (see p. 305).

The last sixty lots of the sale were devoted to Biedermeier and later nineteenth-
century wares; a beaker with silhouettes of the Grand Duke Karl-August of Saxe-
Weimar and his wife, fetched the highest price ever paid for a piece of this type at
auction (see above). In total, the sale of 239 lots made £862,466 ($1,198,828).

A *schwarzlot* beaker decorated by Johann Schaper, Nuremberg, *circa* 1660–70, height 4⅛in (10.5cm)
London £66,000 ($91,740). 16.VI.84
From the collection of Mr and Mrs Fritz Biemann

The continuous scene of a gypsy cavalcade is taken from two plates in a series of engravings by
Jacques Callot, *Les Bohémiens*, published in 1621 (see black and white illustration).

A German gilt roemer, probably Rhenish, *circa* 1620, height 9¼in (23.5cm)
London £49,500 ($68,805). 16.VI.84
From the collection of Mr and Mrs Fritz Biemann

A Netherlandish engraved roemer, seventeenth century, height 10in (25.5cm)
London £26,400 ($36,696). 16.VI.84
From the collection of Mr and Mrs Fritz Biemann

The dwarfs are taken from a series of prints titled *Facétieuses inventions d'amour et de guerre*, probably by François Collignon (1611– 85), a pupil of Jacques Callot.

The Applewhaite-Abbott silkworm letter-weight

T. H. Clarke

Paperweight collecting has come of age. On 2 December 1983 a single paperweight from the Jokelson Collection was sold for a six-figure sum in New York (Fig. 1); this sale was as significant as that of Mrs Applewhaite-Abbott's collection in Sotheby's New Bond Street Rooms on 1 July 1952, when for the first time a single weight was sold for over £1,000, to the applause of an astounded audience. Of even greater moment, perhaps, was the accolade awarded to these technical and visual delights by the exhibition in 1978 at the Corning Glass Museum, 'Paperweights: "Flowers which clothe the meadows"'. This was the first time that a major museum had displayed paperweights as masterpieces of glass. Finally dismissed was the traditional belief that they were simply the spare-time work of the glass manipulator. Indeed, as we now know, paperweights were one of the best-selling lines of the French glass industry from 1845 to about 1860, particularly in the three factories of Baccarat, St Louis and Clichy.

A common factor uniting both the Corning exhibition and the two private collections mentioned above was the presence in all three of a unique piece, the celebrated silkworm weight (Fig. 1); the glass dome enlarges a lampwork creation of four silkworms slowly eating through a mulberry leaf, their preferred food. It is the purpose of this note to give as full a history as possible of this particular object, for it is time that the minor and comparatively modern arts received serious attention, while records and memories are still available.

The first recorded private owner of this entomological specimen was Mrs Applewhaite-Abbott. She lived in a large London house, 11 Cumberland Terrace, Regent's Park. There she bought her first weight in 1917 for £1 5s; and duly entered the purchase in a large ledger. Paperweights (or 'letter-weights', as she liked to call them, a term approved by the Oxford Dictionary) formed only a part of a much larger collection of coloured glass. Happily, Mrs Applewhaite-Abbott's *Glass Book*, as she inscribed her inventory of purchases, is now preserved in the library of the Corning Museum. A superficial study shows that 428 paperweights were listed from 1917 to about 1932. When the collection was sold by her daughter in a series of four sales in 1952–53, the number had risen to 492. The prices paid originally seem bordering on the ridiculous today. The cheapest purchase was 2s. Only 27 out of the 428 cost £10 or more. The highest price was paid in 1931 for '1 Weight Lizzard [*sic*] Very Large Green . . . Very Very rare, £35', now in the Corning Museum. In the same extract from the *Glass Book* (Fig. 2) figures the subject of this article: 'No. 421 1 Weight Silk Worms on Leaf Blue and White Laticino very rare ground (Delosomone) £26'.

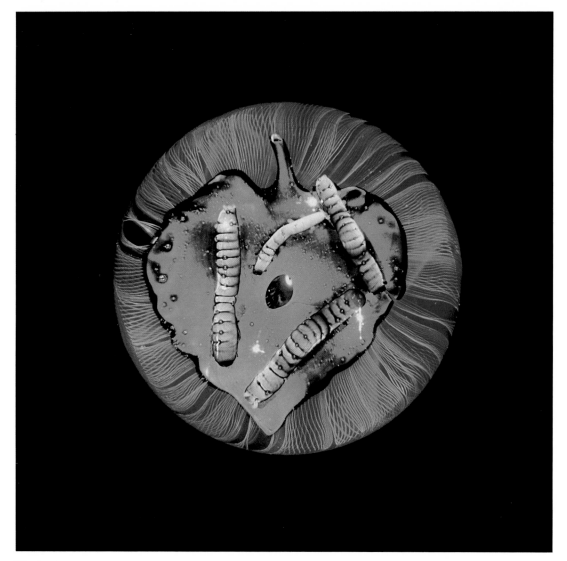

Fig. 1
The Applewhaite-Abbott silkworm weight, diameter 3⅝in (9.2cm)
New York $143,000(£102,878). 2.XII.83
From the collection of Paul Jokelson

Fig. 2
Detail of Mrs Applewhaite-Abbott's *Glass Book*, showing the entry for the silkworm weight
Reproduced courtesy of the Corning Museum of Glass, New York

Fortunately, Mr Bernard Perret of the well-known glass and porcelain dealers, Delomosne (not Delosomone), has total recall of the events leading up to the sale. In 1931, he was offered a paperweight from the Isle of Wight by a runner. From the telephoned description, Perret was unable to decide whether to buy for the high asking price of £5. In the event, the runner came to London and was given £6. Within a few days, the silkworm weight had been sold to Mrs Applewhaite-Abbott for a seemingly large, but absolutely justified, profit of 333.333% recurring: for £26.

At the sale in 1952, the weight was described by the cataloguer, with singular lack of imagination, as 'four mushroom-coloured caterpillars . . . on a dew-bespattered green leaf'. But in attributing a factory he was more sensible: 'perhaps Clichy'. At £1,200 it was the second most expensive weight in the sale. As for the attribution, this is still a matter of controversy in paperweight circles. At the 1983 sale it was described as 'Pantin', a Parisian glass-house only known as a maker of paperweights from the gift of a 'presse-papiers, fleurs et salamandre', in 1880, to the Museum of the Conservatoire des Arts et Métiers in Paris. This weight has long been missing from their collection, but Dwight Lanmon, Corning's director, has discovered a salamander in the round at this Museum, which he believes to be from the Pantin glasshouse. However, Parisian collectors and dealers are sceptical. There *may* be Pantin salamander weights, but to extend this denomination to silkworms arouses their ire and there were protests at the New York sale – not that these had any influence on the price.

To continue the story of the Applewhaite-Abbott silkworm weight, the buyer at Sotheby's on 1 July 1952 was the old-established firm of Spink's. Their client was King Farouk, a passionate collector of watches, stamps, coins, Fabergé, gold boxes, Egyptian antiquities and outmoded aspirin packets, as well as safety razor blades. Omnivorous and indiscriminate in so many of his interests, he was a natural for the nascent paperweight fever. But a bare three weeks after the sale, a burst of Bren-gun fire in Alexandria toppled him from his throne. Paperweight values dropped drastically and Spink's were landed with the second highest-priced paperweight. However, they bided their time and eventually disposed of it to an American fruit grower and collector, Mr Palmer Hart. When Palmer Hart died within a short time, his whole collection was acquired by Mr Paul Jokelson.

It is fitting that the name of the earliest English collector of *presse-papiers*, Mrs Applewhaite-Abbott, should be associated with her record-breaking silkworms, just as the St Louis encased yellow-overlay will forever be associated with the name of Mr Maurice Lindon. Not that this belittles the many achievements of Paul Jokelson, the doyen of Franco-American paperweight enthusiasts. He has collected and written about the paperweights of many nationalities and, as well as being a considerable authority on the art of cameo encrustations or sulphides, he will be remembered for founding and editing *The Annual Bulletin of the Paperweight Collectors' Association*. Beyond that, he has encouraged the making of modern glass weights, not only by the factories of Baccarat and St Louis, but even more by the individual glass artist. The sale of only a part of his collection last December was a testimony to his unique position in the paperweight world.

Left
A St Louis encased
double-overlay
weight,
diameter $3\frac{1}{4}$in (8.2cm)
$39,600 (£28,489)

Right
A Clichy garlanded
plaque weight,
diameter $3\frac{1}{8}$in (7.9cm)
$41,800 (£30,072)

Right
A salamander weight,
possibly Pantin,
diameter $3\frac{7}{8}$in (9.8cm)
$61,600 (£44,317)

Left
A St Louis crown
weight,
diameter $3\frac{1}{4}$in (8.2cm)
$6,875 (£4,946)

Right
A Baccarat primrose
weight,
diameter 3in (7.6cm)
$9,900 (£7,122)

The paperweights illustrated on this page are from the collection of Paul Jokelson and were sold in
New York on 2 December 1983.

Nineteenth-century decorative arts

A St Petersburg Imperial Porcelain Manufactory vase, painted by Fedor I. Krasovsky, signed, factory mark for Nicholas I in underglaze blue, dated *1841*, height $50\frac{3}{8}$in (128cm)
London £24,200 ($33,638). 8.III.84

Fedor Ivanovich Krasovsky (1820–63) was born into a family of state-owned peasants. He trained as a porcelain painter under C. A. Lippold and, at the Imperial Porcelain Manufactory, specialized in flower and fruit subjects. He became a Master Painter in 1850 and was made a Free Artist by the Imperial Academy in 1861.

From left to right
A German ivory tankard, late nineteenth century, height 20⅛in (51.2cm)
London £9,900($13,761). 7.VI.84
One of a pair of ivory ewers, possibly German, *circa* 1875, height 20¼in (51.5cm)
London £9,350($12,997). 7.VI.84

A Viennese silver and hardstone jewel casket, maker's mark of Vincenz Czokally, for Würbel & Czokally, 1883, height 24⅜in (61.9cm)
New York $66,000 (£47,482). 15.XII.83

An associated document written by Friedrich Wilhelm, Crown Prince of Germany, records that this piece was presented to him and his wife by the Emperor Franz Joseph and Empress Elizabeth of Austria for their silver wedding in 1883. The theme of the casket is marriage: the finial symbolizes love and the figures at the angles probably represent charity, fidelity, peace and motherhood.

A pair of French silver wine coolers, maker's mark *ML/Cie*, *circa* 1910, height 12⅜in (31.5cm)
London £35,200 ($48,928). 10.XI.83

These coolers are said to have been made for the Maharajah of Kashmir.

Following page
A Milanese ebony cabinet inlaid with ivory, hardstone and pietra paesina, stamped *Ferd. Pogliani*,
circa 1860, height 9ft 6in (290cm)
London £55,000 ($76,450). 8.VI.84

Ferdinando Pogliani was active in Milan from 1854 and became the city's leading cabinetmaker. He
worked from premises in the fashionable Via Montenapoleone. His use here of semi-precious stones
and bronze ornaments is typical of luxurious Milanese furniture in the late nineteenth century.

See over, p. 315
A Viennese silver and brass-mounted ebony and parcel-gilt cabinet-on-stand inlaid with pietra-dura
by Bernhard Ludwig, *circa* 1880, height 11ft 3in (343cm)
London £115,500 ($160,545). 8.VI.84
From the collection of Mrs Hanreich

According to tradition, only two other cabinets were made; these were given to the King of Romania
and are now in Schloss Sinai.

A French gilt-bronze-mounted boulle commode, inscribed and dated *Henry Dasson 1881*,
width 4ft 1in (124.5cm)
London £37,400 ($51,986). 9.XII.83
From the collection of the late Paul Wallraf

This is a copy of one of a pair of commodes supplied by André-Charles Boulle for the Grand Trianon in
1708–1709, both of which are now at Versailles.

Opposite
A Roman ebony exhibition cabinet-on-stand inlaid with mother-of-pearl, ivory and semi-precious
stones, by Giovanni Battista Gatti, inscribed and dated *1870*, height 5ft 2in (157.5cm)
London £55,000 ($76,450). 8.VI.84

Giovanni Battista Gatti was outstanding among the Italian nineteenth-century craftsmen specializing
in marquetry work. His clients included the Austrian emperor.

Nineteenth-century sculpture

Robert Bowman

In recent years, the art market has moved forward to embrace new areas. However, while Victorian painting, Art Nouveau and Contemporary art have become established collectors' fields at Sotheby's and elsewhere, nineteenth-century sculptors have often been ignored. In the past season, the combination of increased academic interest in the period and a number of specialist sales has begun to change this.

In November 1983, a full-size white marble figure of the *Tinted Venus* by John Gibson made the remarkable price of £68,200 (Fig. 1), as compared with another version of the subject that sold at Sotheby's Belgravia in October 1971 for £2,400. Gibson was commissioned to execute a marble figure of Venus by Joseph Neeld in 1849, but before it was finished Mr and Mrs Robert Preston of Liverpool ordered a replica. This replica, the figure sold in 1971, became the so-called *Tinted Venus*, shown at the International Exhibition of 1862, whose hair, fruit and robe were 'tinted' with gold and red wax, an unusual treatment that received mixed reviews from contemporaries. The statue sold last November was also highlighted in this way.

In the same sale were a superb pair of figures by the English New School sculptor, painter and designer, William Reynolds Stephens (Fig. 2). They clearly show the influence of Sir Alfred Gilbert and George Frampton and are an excellent illustration of the ideas of the New School and the Pre-Raphaelite movement.

'Animalier' bronzes have also been popular, especially decorative casts by better-known artists. In March a classic horse and jockey group by Pierre-Jules Mêne realized £7,150 (Fig. 3). A one-owner sale in Monaco of casts by Antoine-Louis Barye attracted strong bidding, with the numbered casts in particular attaining high prices. Here, decorative objects were less in demand than the more powerful and violent subjects (Fig. 4).

Continental sculptors, like Odoardo Tabacchi and Henri-Louis Cordier (Figs 5–6), have been the subject of a major upturn in interest. Tabacchi worked in the Milanese tradition of strict naturalism and received commissions for several public monuments, including the Cavor Monument in the Piazza Cavor, Milan. He ran a large and successful studio, and was the author of such virtuoso pieces as *Tuffolina*, or *The Bather* (Fig. 5). Carved from a single piece of marble, the life-size figure is superbly modelled; even to the curvature of the button-holes as she prepares to dive. The piece set a new price level for the sculptor, but in future years it may well seem as undervalued as the *Tinted Venus* of 1971.

Fig. 1
A marble figure of the *Tinted Venus*, highlighted with gold and red wax, by John
Gibson, RA, signed and inscribed in Greek, 1851– 56, height of figure 69in (175.4cm)
London £68,200 ($94,798). 22.XI.83
From the collection of the Earl of Altamont

Fig. 2
A pair of bronze, ivory, mother-of-pearl and enamel figures, *Sir Lancelot and the nestling* and
Guinevere and the nestling, by William Reynolds Stephens, RA, each signed, titled and dated
1899, height of figures 32½in (82.5cm) and 34in (86.3cm)
London £45,100 ($62,689). 22.XI.83

Opposite
Fig. 4
A bronze group of a panther attacking a stag by Antoine-Louis Barye, signed, *circa* 1840,
length 20⅞in (53cm)
Monte Carlo FF199,800(£17,194:$23,814). 5.III.84

Fig. 3
A bronze study of a horse and jockey by Pierre-Jules Mêne, signed and dated *1863*,
height 16½in (41.9cm)
London £7,150($9,939). 8.III.84

Fig. 5
A marble figure of *Tuffolina* by Odoardo Tabacchi, *circa* 1895, height of
figure 62in (157.5cm)
London £10,450 ($14,526). 10.XI.83

Fig. 6
A marble figure of *Nymphoea* by Henri-Louis Cordier, signed, titled and dated *1906*,
height of figure 70in (177.7cm)
London £9,350($12,997). 10.XI.83

Art Nouveau and Art Deco

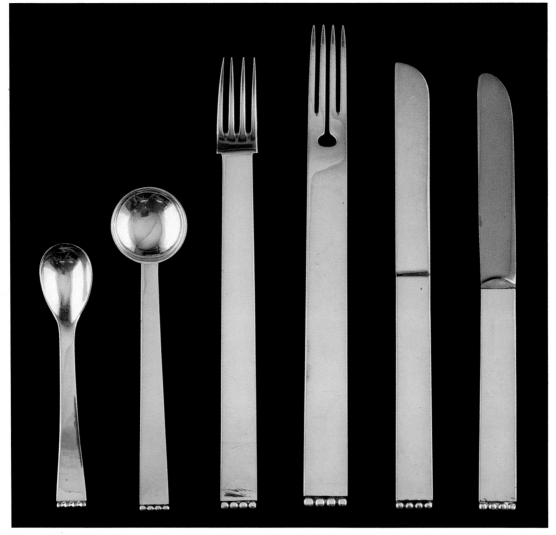

A set of Wiener Werkstätte silver cutlery designed by Josef Hoffmann, *circa* 1904,
maximum length 7⅝in (19.3cm)
Monte Carlo FF177,600 (£15,284:$21,168). 11.III.84

This cutlery is of the same pattern as that designed by Hoffmann in 1903 for the patron and
connoisseur, Fritz Warndorfer.

A cherrywood mantel clock inlaid with fruitwood, ebony and ivory, designed by Josef Maria Olbrich, with original movement, *circa* 1902, height $10\frac{1}{2}$in (26.8cm)
London £16,500 ($22,935). 30.XI.83

The clock was presented to the Olbrich family's music teacher on the occasion of her wedding in 1912. It was probably originally among the furnishings of the artist's own house.

A painted wood cabinet decorated with coloured-glass mosaic on panels of silver leaf, designed by
Charles Rennie Mackintosh, 1902, height 5ft 1in (154.8cm)

This cabinet and four pieces of furniture designed by Mackintosh for the white bedroom of Hous'hill,
home of his patron Miss Cranston, were sold by private treaty to the Royal Ontario Museum, Toronto,
for Can $602,000 (£336,313: $466,667).

Opposite
A Wiener Werkstätte inlaid and jewel-mounted silver vitrine on a macassar and walnut parquetry
base, designed by Carl Otto Czeschka and executed by Josef Czech and Adolf Erbrich, silversmiths,
with Franz Guggenbichler and Josef Holi, metalworkers, height 5ft 4½in (163.5cm)
New York $275,000 (£197,842). 19.XI.83

This vitrine was exhibited at the Vienna 'Kunstschau' in 1908, where it was bought by Karl Wittgenstein.
It is among the most elaborate pieces of furniture produced by the Wiener Werkstätte.

The conquest of the horse, a lacquered-plaster panel designed by Jean Dunand, signed, *circa* 1934,
59in by 71in (149.8cm by 180.5cm)
New York $73,700 (£53,022). 12.V.84

This is a reduced version of one of four monumental lacquered walls executed for the first-class
smoking room of the SS *Normandie*. Dunand's commission was on the theme *The pursuits of mankind*;
the other panels were entitled *The harvest*, *Fishing* and *The dance*.

Opposite
An ebony cabinet inlaid with mother-of-pearl, abalone and silver designed by Süe et Mare,
1927, height 5ft $1\frac{7}{8}$in (157cm)
Monte Carlo FF1,443,000 (£124,182: $171,990). 11.III.84

This cabinet was among the furnishings of Jane Renouardt's villa at St-Cloud, designed by Louis Süe
in 1927.

A Morris and Co. Hammersmith rug designed by John Henry Dearle for Stanmore Hall, Middlesex, *circa* 1895, 19ft 8in by 13ft (599cm by 396cm). London £41,800 ($58,102). 13.IV.84

A stoneware vase by Hans Coper, impressed *HC* seal,
circa 1970, height 20½in (52cm)
London £14,300 ($19,877). 30.XI.83

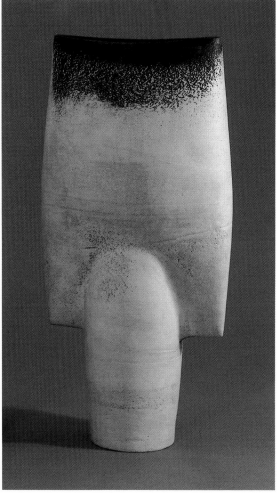

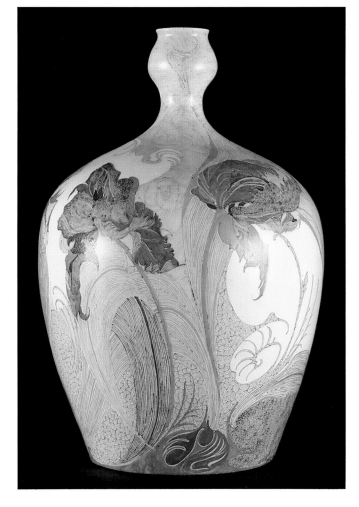

A Rozenburg egg-shell earthenware vase decorated
by Samuel Schellinck, printed mark *Rozenburg den
Haag* and painted artist's monogram, 1902
height 9¼in (23.5cm)
London £9,350 ($12,997). 13.IV.84

Jewellery

A step-cut emerald and diamond tiara, last quarter nineteenth century
London £10,450($14,526). 8.III.84

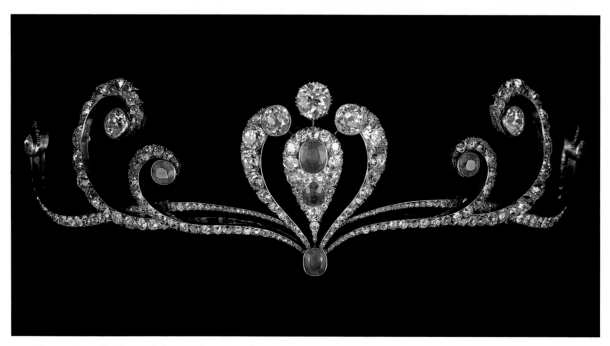

A cushion-shaped ruby and diamond tiara, *circa* 1870
London £33,000($45,870). 15.XII.83

Above A pearl and diamond stomacher brooch, mid-nineteenth century. London £9,900 ($13,761).24.V.84
Below A diamond necklace, last quarter nineteenth century. London £6,820 ($9,480). 24.V.84

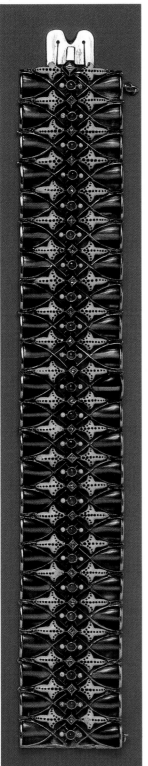

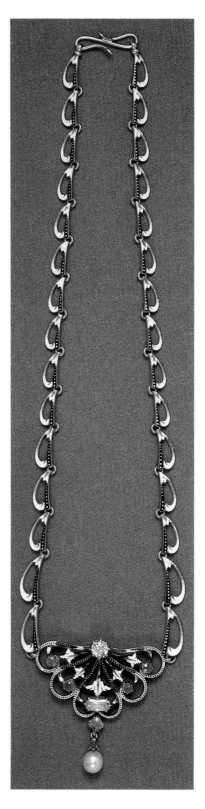

Opposite
A garnet and diamond necklace
Geneva SFr44,000 (£14,058:$19,469).
17.XI.83

This necklace was formerly in the
private collection of the late Queen Maria
Cristina of Spain.

Left
A gold, enamel and jewelled bracelet
by Giuliano, *circa* 1865
London £10,450 ($14,526). 24.V.84

Right
A gold, enamel and jewelled necklace
by Giuliano, *circa* 1890
London £4,620 ($6,422). 24.V.84

Above A black onyx, emerald and diamond panther bracelet by Cartier
New York $132,000 (£94,964). 12.IV.84
Below A black onyx, coral, emerald and diamond panther brooch by Cartier
New York $68,750 (£49,460). 12.IV.84

In 1922, Louis Cartier, inspired by a visit to Africa, called together a team of setters and lapidaries to create his famous 'panther' jewellery.

Opposite
An Art Deco ruby and diamond necklace with a detachable pendant, *circa* 1930
New York $55,000 (£39,568). 14.VI.84

A black pearl and diamond necklace with a pair of black pearl and diamond earrings
New York $110,000 (£79,137). 12.IV.84

The necklace and earrings were owned formerly by Eleanor 'Cissy' Patterson, a member of the great
newspaper family. As well as being a celebrated society hostess and novelist, she was for nine years the
editor of the *Washington Herald*, which she later merged with the *Washington Times*.

A sapphire and diamond bracelet by Van Cleef & Arpels, 1938
New York $209,000(£150,360). 12.IV.84
From the collection of Palm Beach Atlantic College

Above A horn, pearl, ruby and diamond clip by Cartier. St Moritz SFr104,500(£33,387:$46,239). 25.II.84
Below A diamond necklace by Cartier. St Moritz SFr572,000(£182,748:$253,097). 25.II.84

A diamond necklace and bracelet. St Moritz SFr121,000 (£38,658: $53,540). 25.II.84

Kashmir sapphires

Michael O'Donoghue

Sapphire has always been considered one of the most valuable and desirable of gemstones. The word 'sapphire' probably derives from a Sanskrit word for the colour blue; but the gem species corundum, of which sapphire is a member, also accounts for the red of ruby and yellow, orange, pink, green and even colourless varieties. The unique velvety cornflower blue of the finest sapphires from the province of Kashmir makes them particularly desirable (see opposite). The mines are remote in the Himalayas and the great rarity of stones from this region has further enhanced their value. In fact, commercially, the establishment of the origin of a gemstone has become almost as important as the classification of its quality; often, experts will differ as to quality, whereas the material contained in a stone will frequently make its place of origin clear beyond doubt.

Kashmir sapphires come from the Paddar region of the country. The deposit is similar geologically to that of the Hunza valley in Pakistan, known to produce fine ruby. The mineralogy of the Paddar deposit consists of marbles in strata, intermingled with masses of dark biotite mica, some of which contain garnet crystals. The strata of marble are also intruded by feldspathic pegmatites and, providing that silica is absent, sapphire forms in these locations in some profusion. Prospectors look for decomposed feldspar, which is found in pockets that may be 1 metre thick and 2 to 4 metres long. The decomposed feldspar is in fact the china clay so familiar to Cornishmen.

There are several mines in the area, of which the Old Mine probably produced the best stones. This mine, like most of the others, lies at a considerable altitude (14,775 feet), so that access is difficult for both workers and visitors; snow and ice bar the way for much of the year. In the New Mines a pink variety of corundum is found as well as the blue. Sapphire is also found in the streams and beds on the valley floor, although apparently these placer deposits are not worked today.

An examination of Kashmir sapphire shows that virtually all specimens contain a banding of colour. Under the microscope, the bands can be seen to consist of layers of liquid inclusions; these are assemblies of minute liquid-filled tubes and the general effect over the whole stone is one of velvety 'sleepiness', the traditional name given to this effect by the trade. The blue colour is more pure than that of blue sapphires from other locations, such as Australia and Sri Lanka. Sri Lanka tends to produce blue stones with a very irregular distribution of colour and Australian stones incline to steeliness or inkiness. Kashmir sapphires retain their fine blue colour under a variety of different lighting conditions.

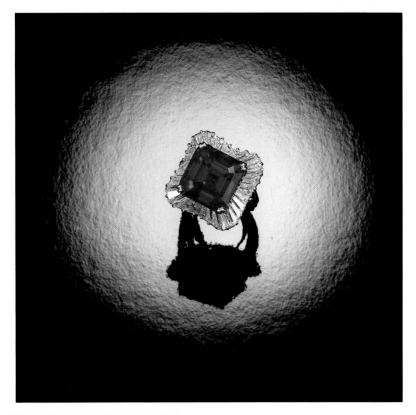

An emerald-cut Kashmir sapphire
(28.18 carats) and diamond ring
New York $671,000(£482,734). 19.X.83

A cushion-shaped Kashmir sapphire
(22.18 carats) and diamond ring
New York $506,000(£364,029). 19.X.83

The gemmologist cannot distinguish Kashmir stones from those found in other localities if he applies only the basic tests of refractive index and specific gravity. Examination under the microscope is essential. In a Kashmir sapphire, apart from the colour zoning already mentioned, there are flat films containing a brownish or yellowish liquid. As in sapphires from Sri Lanka, structures made up of liquid-filled tubes, the whole resembling a fingerprint, can be found; but more characteristic of Kashmir sapphire are black crystals, which are probably tourmaline. This is not unlikely, since some of the deposits yield tourmaline crystals, a feature of pegmatite pockets. Other included crystals are also found in sapphires from elsewhere, so they are not particularly indications of a Kashmir origin. The liquid-filled films, the zoning and the general air of sleepiness should together be considered fairly clear proof that a stone has come from Kashmir.

The Kashmir sapphire deposits are not well known in history. The first serious survey of the area was carried out in 1887 by T. D. La Touche, who sent a report to the Geological Survey of India. During his survey the largest stone of note was found, a parti-coloured sapphire of 933 carats. The first stones to reach commercial outlets had probably been exposed by a landslide as far back as 1881. By 1882 crystals were turning up in Simla and being bought by merchants. It is known that Tibetans traded salt for sapphires and conducted their bargaining on a weight by weight basis. This would be less commercially sensible today! Troops were sent by the Maharajah of Kashmir to guard the mine, no doubt an early attempt to prevent smuggling, so it is clear that the quality of the crystals must have been highly regarded from the first. The best and largest crystals were found between 1883 and 1887; an attempt in 1888 by La Touche to uncover new sources failed. Perhaps he was too ambitious; his idea was to start a fresh landslide. By 1906 a private firm, the Kashmir Mining Company, had become involved in the recovery of sapphires and some of the originally worked placer deposits were re-examined, yielding further fine specimens.

Work on the mines has never been much more than sporadic, the climate and the altitude preventing concerted effort. Sapphires were recovered through the 'twenties and 'thirties, but the Second World War caused production to fall to a low level. From 1952 to 1959 the Kashmir government worked the mines, but their operations are said to have run at a loss, and no one else has been allowed to work in the area.

Today there seems to be no mining taking place. The area is guarded and although sapphires were sold at state government auctions up to 1969, none have been held since that year. Local people find a few stones, some of which make their way to Delhi, but apparently more reach such centres as Hong Kong and Switzerland than the traditional Indian gem centre of Jaipur. There can be little doubt that the meagre supply of Kashmir sapphires in recent years has helped to sustain the demand for this beautiful gemstone.

REFERENCES
D. Atkinson and R. Z. Kothavala, 'Kashmir sapphire', *Gems & Gemology*, 19 (2) 1983
T. D. La Touche, 'The sapphire mines of Kashmir', *Records of the Geological Survey of India*, 23, 1890
R. V. Gaines, 'The Kashmir sapphire mines', *Himalayan Journal*, 13, 1946
C. S. Middlemiss, 'Precious and semi-precious gemstones of Jammu and Kashmir', *Mineral survey reports, Jammu and Kashmir government*, 1931, etc

Left
An emerald-cut light-pink diamond (16.4 carats)
New York $346,500 (£249,281). 12.IV.84

Right
A cushion-shaped diamond (28.69 carats) ring
London £46,200 ($64,218). 15.XII.83

An emerald-cut sapphire
(27.52 carats) and
diamond ring by Tiffany
New York $242,000
(£174,101). 12.IV.84

A brilliant-cut fancy blue
diamond (2.79 carats)
New York $96,250
(£69,245). 12.IV.84

A pair of diamond pendent earrings, the pear-shaped
diamonds weighing 10.83 and 10.63 carats
New York $605,000 (£435,252). 14.VI.84

From left to right
An emerald-cut diamond (22.28 carats) ring
New York $583,000 (£419,424). 8.XII.83
A cushion-shaped sapphire (50.88 carats)
Geneva SFr 1,210,000 (£386,581: $535,398).
17.XI.83

From left to right
A heart-shaped diamond (18.22 carats) ring
St Moritz SFr 990,000 (£316,294: $438,053). 25.II.84
A step-cut emerald (4.15 carats) and diamond ring
by Cartier
New York $68,750 (£49,460). 12.IV.84

Antiquities and Asian art

A Roman sheet-bronze panel, probably from the side of a chariot, decorated in relief with a charioteer in a quadriga, *circa* first–second century AD, width 23in (58.4cm)
London £30,800 ($42,812). 12.XII.83

A Hellenistic terracotta figure of a woman, *circa* third century BC, height 39½in (100.3cm)
London £16,500 ($22,935). 9.VII.84

An Egyptian quartzite bust of a nobleman, Eighteenth
Dynasty, reign of Tuthmosis IV–Amenhotep III,
1413–1365 BC, height $4\frac{1}{2}$in (11.4cm)
New York $24,200(£17,410). 1.III.84
From the collection of the late Lester Wolfe

A Roman bronze mask of Silenus, first half
first century AD, height $8\frac{1}{4}$in (21cm)
London £24,200($33,638). 12.XII.83
From the collection of the Rt Hon. the Lord Methuen

An Egyptian granite head of Sekhmet from a seated statue of the lion-headed goddess, Eighteenth Dynasty, reign of Amenhotep III, 1403–1365 BC, height 14in (35.5cm) New York $236,500 (£170,144). 1.III.84

Several hundred granite statues of Sekhmet once lined the court and passages of the temple that Amenhotep III built for the goddess Mut at Karnak, near Thebes.

An Egyptian limestone statue of the steward Qar and his wife Khentyses, Fifth–Sixth Dynasty, 2450–2155 BC, height 24in (61cm)
New York $148,500 (£106,835). 1.III.84

An Egyptian limestone relief fragment of Rameses II, Nineteenth Dynasty, *circa* 1290–1280 BC,
height 20in (50.8cm)
New York $66,000 (£47,482). 8.VI.84
From the collection of the late Charles D. Kelekian

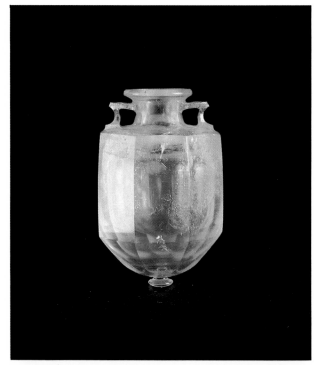

An Egyptian turquoise-glazed faïence sistrum fragment in the form of the janus head of Hathor, the cow-eared goddess, *circa* 600 BC, height $3\frac{1}{8}$ in (7.9cm)
London £16,500 ($22,935). 9.VII.84

Above, right
A Roman rock-crystal amphoriskos, *circa* first–second century AD, height $2\frac{1}{2}$ in (6.4cm)
London £21,450 ($29,816). 12.XII.83
From the collection of the late Thomas F. Flannery, Jr

A Neo-Babylonian terracotta cuneiform barrel cylinder, reign of Nebuchadnezzar II, *circa* 604–561 BC, height $8\frac{5}{8}$ in (22cm)
London £24,200 ($33,638). 12.XII.83

An eastern Indian stone stele depicting Vishnu, late tenth century, height 45½in (115.6cm)
London £12,100 ($16,819). 23.VII.84

Tribal art

A Bwiti copper, brass-wire and wood reliquary figure, Gabon, nineteenth century, height 18¾in (47.5cm)
London £69,300 ($96,327). 25.VI.84

A Mangbetu bark and wood container for honey,
Zaïre, inscribed, nineteenth century,
height 21⅛in (53.5cm)
London £14,300 ($19,877). 25.VI.84
From the collection of Robert and Helen Kuhn

A Polynesian wood male figure of *moai kava-kava*,
Easter Island, early nineteenth century,
height 18½in (47cm)
New York $22,000 (£15,827). 2.XII.83
From the collection of Mr J. Pike

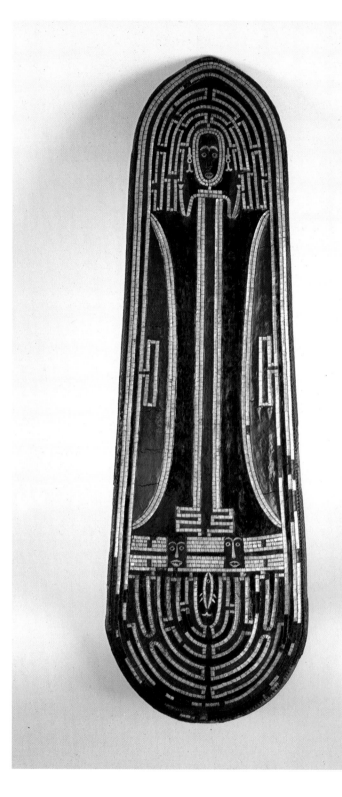

Opposite
A Navajo serape, Classic period,
76in by 50in (193cm by 127cm)
New York $115,500 (£83,094). 22.X.83

Left
A Melanesian wickerwork ceremonial
shield painted with coloured resin and
inlaid with mother-of-pearl, Florida,
Solomon Islands, nineteenth century,
height 36½in (92.7cm)
New York $253,000 (£182,014).
2.XII.83

Twenty long elliptical wickerwork
shields decorated with mother-of-pearl
or nautilus shell are known to exist;
the combination of this shape and form
of decoration seems to be unique to the
island of Florida. The delicacy of the
shell inlay makes it certain that the
shields were for ceremonial rather than
practical use. The two heads at the feet
of the stylized central figure here
probably represent trophies; the
Solomon Islands were notorious
for head-hunting.

Islamic art

A Syrian moulded and carved pottery stand, Raqqa, twelfth–thirteenth century,
width 12¾in (32.4cm)
London £8,250($11,468). 18.IV.84

A Mamluk underglaze-painted pottery jar, Damascus, fourteenth century, height 16$\frac{3}{8}$in (41.6cm)
New York $30,800 (£22,158). 8.VI.84

A Safavid blue and white pottery dish, seventeenth century, diameter $18\frac{3}{8}$ in (46.7cm)
London £18,700 ($25,993). 18.IV.84

An Isnik blue and white pottery dish, early sixteenth century, diameter 16in (40.6cm)
New York $11,000 (£7,914). 8.VI.84
From the collection of the late Charles D. Kelekian

A north-west Persian compartment carpet, seventeenth century,
15ft 1in by 7ft 4in (460cm by 223.5cm)
London £20,900($29,051). 18.IV.84

An Ottoman hanging, seventeenth–eighteenth century, 6ft 11in by 4ft 1in
(211cm by 124.5cm)
London £5,280($7,339). 19.X.83

A Ghashghai saddle rug, last quarter nineteenth century, 3ft 5in by 2ft 9in (104cm by 84cm)
New York $9,900(£7,122). 19.V.84
From the collection of the Austin family

A Beshir prayer rug, *circa* 1880, 5ft 10in by 3ft 7in (178cm by 109cm)
New York $22,000(£15,827). 5.XI.83

A Kum Kapour silk and metal-thread prayer rug, *circa* 1900, 5ft 8in by 3ft 8in
(172cm by 111cm)
Geneva SFr165,000 (£52,716: $73,009). 15.V.84

A Heriz silk carpet, signed by Sabbagh, *circa* 1875, 10ft 3in by 8ft 4in (312.5cm by 254cm)
New York $165,000 (£118,705). 19.V.84

Chinese art

An archaic bronze cauldron (*ding*), Shang–early Western Zhou Dynasty, diameter 6½in (16.5cm)
London £176,000 ($244,640). 19.VI.84

An inlaid archaic bronze box and cover (*fangyi*), eleventh–tenth century BC, height 7½in (19.1cm)
London £181,500 ($252,285). 19.VI.84

A bronze ewer, sixth century, height 9in (22.9cm)
New York $96,250 (£69,245). 7.XII.83

Two views of an engraved parcel-gilt silver bowl, Tang Dynasty, diameter 9½in (24.2cm)
New York $187,000 (£134,532). 7.XII.83

The collection of Mr and Mrs Richard C. Bull

A gilt-bronze and turquoise sleeve-weight in the form of a *qilin*,
Han Dynasty, height 2⅜in (6cm)
New York $137,500(£98,921). 6.XII.83
From the collection of Mr and
Mrs Richard C. Bull

One of the most important private collections of archaic Chinese art, that of Mr and Mrs Richard C. Bull of Villanova, Pennsylvania, was auctioned by Sotheby's in New York on 6 December 1983. Mr Bull's attention was first directed towards the early period as a result of his friendship with Dr Alfred Salmony, Professor of Oriental Art at the Institute of Fine Arts in New York. Formed over some forty years, the collection featured archaic jade, ceremonial bronze vessels and other archaeological material, including objects dating from the Neolithic period. Many of the best pieces have been displayed in exhibitions around the world.

The Bull Collection was especially rich in archaic belthooks, an invention of the Warring States period. Among them was a large well-carved jade example with a pendent mask (see opposite), which established an auction record for jade. Other highlights of the sale included a fine archaic bronze food vessel (*liding*) from the Shang Dynasty (see p. 374), superbly cast with powerful ram's head masks in high relief above each leg. Early gilt bronzes also attracted attention, particularly a tortoise-form appliqué dating from the Han Dynasty, which was engraved and gilt in two tones to highlight the subtle design, and a *qilin*-form sleeve-weight with bulging turquoise eyes (see above). These weights were used to keep the sleeves of robes in place in tombs.

In total, the sale of 286 lots made $2,446,832 (£1,760,311).

An archaic jade belthook and pendent two-sided *taotie* mask, Warring States period,
length 7⅜in (18.7cm)
New York $396,000 (£284,892). 6.XII.83
From the collection of Mr and Mrs Richard C. Bull

An archaic bronze ritual vessel (*liding*), Shang Dynasty, height 9in (22.8cm)
New York $209,000 (£150,360). 6.XII.83
From the collection of Mr and Mrs Richard C. Bull

A Neolithic jade ceremonial blade, length $12\frac{7}{8}$in (32.7cm)
New York $132,000(£94,964). 6.XII.83
From the collection of Mr and Mrs Richard C. Bull

A marble figure of a hare, Tang Dynasty, length 8in (20.3cm)
New York $104,500(£75,180). 6.XII.83
From the collection of Mr and Mrs Richard C. Bull

A pair of *sancai* glazed pottery tomb guardians, Tang Dynasty, height 40in (101.6cm) and 39½in (100.3cm)
New York $286,000 (£205,755). 12.VI.84
From the collection of John W. Gruber

It is likely that these figures were excavated from the same tomb, probably near Xian (Shaanxi province), site of the Tang capital.

A *sancai* glazed pottery seated figure, Tang Dynasty, height 13⅝in (34.6cm)
London £118,800($165,132). 19.VI.84

A moulded Guanyao basin (*xi*),
Southern Song Dynasty,
diameter $7\frac{7}{8}$in (20cm)
Hong Kong HK$2,750,000
(£253,924:$352,113). 14.XI.83

A Geyao censer, Song Dynasty,
diameter $4\frac{7}{8}$in (12.3cm)
London £132,000($183,480). 13.XII.83

A Cizhou *meiping*, Song–Yuan Dynasty, height 8½in (21.6cm)
London £31,900 ($44,341). 13.XII.83

A Ming blue and white dish, late fourteenth century, diameter 14$\frac{3}{8}$in (36.5cm)
Hong Kong HK$1,210,000(£111,727:$154,930). 21.V.84

A Ming blue and white stemcup with copper-red decoration, Chenghua, diameter 6½in (16.5cm) Hong Kong HK$1,320,000 (£121,884:$169,014). 14.XI.83

Two views of a Ming white-glazed engraved ewer, Yongle, height 7¾in (19.8cm) Hong Kong HK$935,000 (£86,334:$119,718). 14.XI.83

A pair of enamelled export figures of leopards, Kangxi, length 40in (101.6cm)
Monte Carlo FF1,443,000(£124,182:$171,990), 27.VI.84
From the collection of the late Florence J. Gould

A pair of enamelled export goose tureens and covers, Qianlong, height 15¾in (40cm)
London £50,600 ($70,334). 3.VII.84

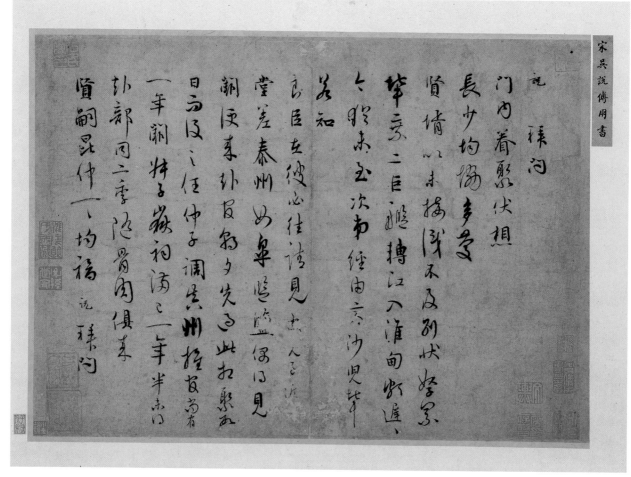

An album of calligraphy, comprising *Notes by Song People* and *Genuine Works by Famous Yuan Worthies*, twenty-five leaves, ink on paper, with 193 seals and later colophons, Song and Yuan Dynasties
New York $297,000 (£213,669). 13.VI.84

Opposite
A wood figure of Guanyin, twelfth–thirteenth century, height 56¼in (142.9cm)
Monte Carlo FF1,110,000 (£95,525: $132,300). 27.VI.84
From the collection of the late Florence J. Gould

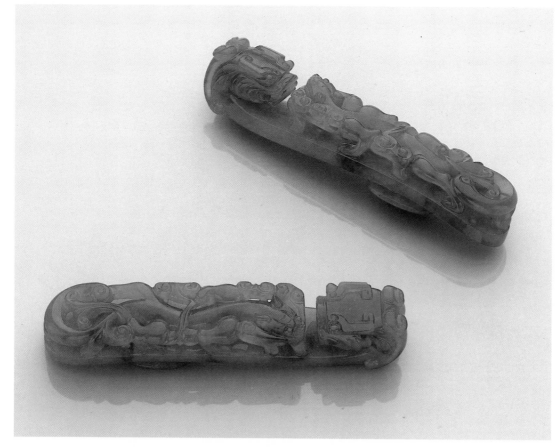

A pair of Imperial jadeite belthooks, length 3¾in (9.5cm)
Hong Kong HK$2,750,000 (£253,924: $352,113). 15.XI.83

Opposite
An Imperial cloisonné-enamel censer and cover, Qianlong, height 55in (139.7cm)
Monte Carlo FF888,000 (£76,420: $105,840). 4.III.84

Lord Loch of Drylaw brought this piece back from China in 1861, following the sack of the Summer Palace the year before.

An Imperial enamelled glass snuff
bottle, four character mark and
period of Qianlong
New York $44,000 (£31,655).
15.III.84
From the collection of Mei Ling

A cinnabar lacquer snuff bottle,
incised seal mark of Qianlong
London £12,650 ($17,584).
2.VII.84

An Imperial ivory snuff bottle,
incised mark and period of
Qianlong
New York $33,000 (£23,741).
15.III.84
From the collection of Mei Ling

An Imperial enamelled ruby-ground bowl, four character mark Kangxi yuzhi and of the period,
diameter 4⅜in (11cm)
Hong Kong HK$528,000 (£48,753:$67,606). 15.XI.83

CHINESE SCHOOL
An album of 150 watercolours, *circa* 1810, page size 18½in by 14½in
(47cm by 36.9cm)
New York $181,500 (£130,576). 17.III.84

This is one of eighty-one flower pictures in the album; other subjects include
court figures, insects, fish, birds, vegetables, fruit and nuts.

Japanese art

A lacquer flask decorated with Portuguese figures, Momoyama period, height $6\frac{1}{4}$in (15.7cm)
London £7,150($9,939). 19.X.83
Now in the Ashmolean Museum, Oxford

A gold lacquer cabinet, Meiji period, height 23in (58.6cm)
London £9,900($13,761). 19.X.83

A lacquer *bundai* and *suzuribako*, late Edo–Meiji period, length of *bundai* 25⅝in (65.1cm), width of *suzuribako* 9¾in (24.7cm)
New York $24,200(£17,410). 31.III.84

A pair of cloisonné-enamel vases, Meiji period, height 60¼in (153cm)
New York $26,400 (£18,993). 31.III.84

A silver-mounted cloisonné-enamel vase and cover by Namikawa Yasuyuki,
signed *Kyoto, Namikawa*, Meiji period, height 6⅛in (15.5cm)
London £15,950($22,171). 19.X.83

A clock garniture by Miyao, signed, Meiji period, height of clock 48¾in (123.8cm)
New York $60,500 (£43,525). 31.III.84

An ivory *netsuke* of a Dutchman,
eighteenth century
London £5,280 ($7,339). 14.III.84
From the collection of the late
Miss M.A. Beasley

An ivory *netsuke* of a tigress and
cub by Tomotada, signed, Kyoto,
eighteenth century
London £18,700 ($25,993). 19.X.83

Left
A wood *netsuke* of a *kirin* by
Masakata, signed, Kyoto,
late eighteenth century
London £22,000 ($30,580). 14.III.84
From the collection of the late
Miss M.A. Beasley

Left
An ivory *netsuke* of a Dutchman,
eighteenth century
London £16,500 ($22,935). 14.III.84
From the collection of the late
Miss M.A. Beasley

Right
An ivory *netsuke* of a Dutchman,
eighteenth century
London £17,050 ($23,700). 14.III.84
From the collection of the late
Miss M.A. Beasley

Left
A lacquer sheath *inro* by
Shiomi Masanari, signed,
nineteenth century
London £5,500 ($7,645).
16.XI.83

Right
A lacquer *inro* by Shibata
Zeshin, signed,
nineteenth century
London £18,700 ($25,993).
16.XI.83

Right
A lacquer *inro* with tan ground by
Kanshosai Toyo, signed, with
kakihan, eighteenth century
London £5,060 ($7,033). 16.XI.83

Left
A lacquer tea scoop with
green *ishime* ground by
Shibata Zeshin, signed,
nineteenth century
London £5,720 ($7,951).
16.XI.83

Right
A gold lacquer *inro* by
Shiomi Masanari, signed,
nineteenth century
London £6,600 ($9,174).
16.XI.83

SOTATSU SCHOOL
Clumps of flowers and plants for the four seasons
A pair of six-panel screens, colour and *gofun* over gold leaf on paper, *Inen* seal, seventeenth–eighteenth century, each panel 69¾in by 25in (177cm by 63.5cm)
London £15,400 ($21,406). 26.IV.84

Opposite
HOKUSAI KATSUSHIKA
Oban, signed
London £3,520 ($4,893). 26.IV.84

This print illustrates a poem by Minamoto Muneyuki Ason: 'The mountain village, deserted in winter, is all the more lonely, with none to visit, and all grass seared to desolation.' It comes from the series *The Hundred Poems as Explained by the Nurse*, circa 1839.

ANDO HIROSHIGE
A sudden summer shower
Oban, signed and inscribed, *circa* 1833. London £4,730($6,575). 9.XI.83

Postage stamps

GREAT BRITAIN, 1855–57
4d carmine on blued paper,
watermark small garter,
unused pair
London £2,640($3,670).
22.IX.83

KENYA, UGANDA AND
TANGANYIKA, 1922–27
£50 black and brown,
unused
London £4,620($6,422).
7.III.84

RHODESIA, 1905 Victoria Falls 1s blue-green, unused strip of three, imperforate vertically,
except between stamp and margin
London £6,600($9,174). 22.IX.83

WESTERN
AUSTRALIA, 1854
4d slate-blue,
transfer variety
P of *PENCE* with
small head, unused
London
£3,960($5,504).
23.IX.83

NYASALAND, 1898 cheque stamps,
1d vermilion and pale ultramarine,
centres omitted, in vertical pairs
with normals, unused block of four
London £4,180($5,810). 22.IX.83
From the collection of
Bryan de Robeck

INDIA, 1854 $\frac{1}{2}$ anna, Die III, unused
corner block of four
London £2,750($3,823). 7.III.84

UNITED STATES OF AMERICA, 1861 Civil War entire letter from New Orleans, addressed to Paris, carried by the Adams Express Company 'across-the-lines' to Louisville, Kentucky, and there put into the United States mail, franked with 1861–62 30¢ orange, tied by Louisville duplex of 22 August
London £12,650 ($17,584). 7.III.84

CYPRUS, 1882 soldier's envelope addressed to England, bearing two 1882 watermark Crown CC $\frac{1}{2}$ on $\frac{1}{2}$ piastre, with manuscript PP and D47 numeral cancellations
London £2,750 ($3,823). 22.IX.83

Collectors' sales

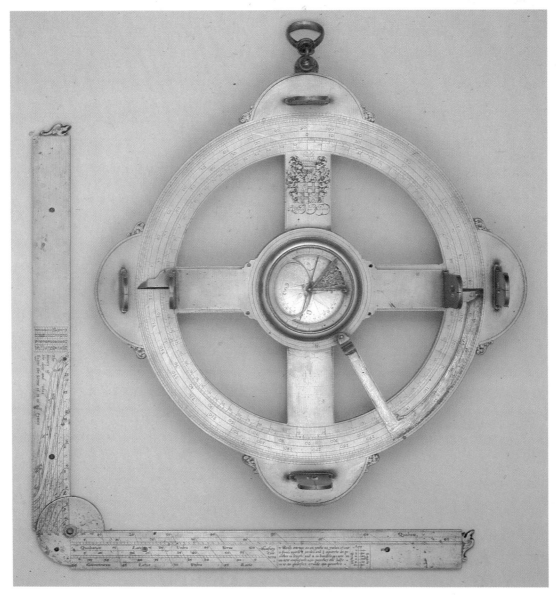

From left to right
A brass surveyor's folding rule by Humfrey Cole, London, signed and dated *1574*,
length folded 12in (30.5cm). London £17,600 ($24,464). 12.VI.84
A brass circumferentor by Henricus Sneewins, signed, Leiden, mid-seventeenth century,
diameter 13in (33cm). London £18,700 ($25,993). 12.VI.84

This circumferentor was made for the Dutch mathematician T. Wapen Van Schooten, Senior. It is
one of the earliest instruments to use the vernier scale, putting into practice a theory first published
by Paul Vernier in 1631.

An American copper and zinc weathervane of an Indian chief, probably New York State,
mid-nineteenth century, height 36in (91.5cm)
New York $41,800 (£30,072). 30.VI.84

A German clockwork open tourer by Carette, *circa* 1910,
length 12½in (31.8cm)
London £6,710($9,327). 17.I.84

This toy was sold with the original cardboard box, bearing a label
inscribed *Gamages 12/6d*.

A German tinplate 'Rocket' gauge 'I' spirit-fired steam locomotive and carriages by Marklin, *circa* 1909
London £28,050($38,990). 29.V.84

An English wood doll in original clothes, *circa* 1690, height 16¾in (42.6cm)
London £17,600 ($24,464). 29.V.84

This doll is the earliest and finest to appear at auction since Lord and Lady Clapham, now in the
Victoria & Albert Museum, London, were sold at Sotheby's in 1974. She is possibly by the same
maker and is in remarkable condition; even her clothes have not faded.

From left to right
A Phantom Vox electric guitar organ used by John Lennon of *The Beatles*, with an authenticating letter signed by George Harrison, *circa* 1965, length 41in (104.2cm). London £8,800 ($12,232). 1.IX.83
A Broadwood upright piano used by John Lennon of *The Beatles*, with an inscribed brass plaque, late nineteenth century, width 53in (134.7cm). London £8,800 ($12,232). 1.IX.83

A 1965 Rolls-Royce Phantom V, with bodywork by Mulliner Park Ward
New York $115,500 (£83,094). 23.VI.84
From the collection of Yoko Ono

A 1928 Rolls-Royce 40/50hp Phantom I, with sedanca de ville bodywork by Hooper
Kilbrittain Castle IR £17,600 (£14,194: $15,714). 5.IX.83

This car is believed to have been exhibited at the Paris Salon. It was purchased by the Duchess of
Westminster and appears to have been little used.

A 1935 Lagonda LG45 4½ litre Rapide open sports tourer
Nostell Priory £20,900 ($29,051). 3.III.84

Wine

A rosewood and yew decanting cradle,
early nineteenth century
London £800 ($1,112). 28.IX.83

From left to right
Château Mouton Rothschild 1945, CB (one bottle)
London £420 ($584). 7.XII.83
Château Latour 1961, CB (an Imperial)
London £2,500 ($3,475). 7.XII.83

The value of wine sales at Sotheby's has grown to the record level of £2.9 million ($4) in the United Kingdom during the season ending July 1984. Sales in Geneva, Johannesburg and Pulborough have added £295,236 ($410,378). At the tenth annual sale of rare Cape wines at Nederburg, the record level of R825,201 (£466,215: $644,688) was reached. The department has also provided the auctioneer at fund-raising events, for the Sonoma County Wine Auction and for a televised sale on behalf of KQED, the public television station in San Francisco.

Sales of port have increased in recent months. Sotheby's has led this field, disposing of well over 5,500 cases. Claret still remains the most popular wine with consumers and investors both in Europe and America; prices have risen by 20 to 50 percent since 1983.

Among significant or record prices this year have been £7,200 for a jeroboam (six bottles) of Château Mouton Rothschild 1929; £1,400 for a dozen bottles of Romanée

From left to right
Madeira Terrantez Vintage 1862, OB, Rutherford and Miles (two bottles)
London £220 ($306). 7.XII.83
Château Lafite 1887, CB (one bottle)
London £240 ($334). 28.IX.83
Château Pétrus 1945, CB (one bottle)
London £720 ($1,001). 28.IX.83
Ferreira 1815, OB (one bottle)
London £250 ($348). 28.IX.83
Château d'Yquem 1921, CB (one bottle)
London £305 ($424). 28.III.84

Right
A Dutch silver pocket corkscrew, *circa* 1800
London £290 ($403). 28.IX.83

Conti 1969; £3,100 for two double magnums of Richebourg 1949; £950 for a dozen bottles of Taylor 1935; £360 for two bottles of Quinta do Noval 1931; £780 for a dozen bottles of Château Lafite 1970; £135 for one bottle of Bastardo 1870 Madeira.

Over the season, the experts in the department have been active. As well as the regular assessment and valuation of stock for the trade and private owners, they have often been called upon to speak to wine societies and students of wine, providing market reports and investment advice. The programme of wine education, begun in 1982, was extended by a tasting of seventy-seven examples of the 1975 vintage, representing the best-known classed growths of Bordeaux.

New wine publications to appear shortly will include *Chablis* by Rosemary George, MW, *Alsace* by Pamela Vandyke Price and *Rioja* by Jan Read, which will complement the popular wine books already in print from Sotheby Publications.

'Treasured Possessions'

Michael Saunders Watson,
President of the Historic Houses Association

A hardened buyer entering the great auction rooms at Sotheby's between 21 December 1983 and 20 January 1984 must have received something of a shock. Gone were the chairs and the auctioneer's rostrum, to be replaced by a splendid miscellany of objects, ranging from a presentation wheelbarrow to a huge scallop-shaped bed, awaiting the birth of Botticelli's Venus; from a full-sized Egyptian mummy-case, reputedly with its occupant still in place, to a Burmese elephant stud-book; and on the walls a remarkable range of pictures from all periods. The effect was that of a magnificent Aladdin's cave. It was, in fact, a special exhibition, 'Treasured Possessions', organized by Sotheby's in conjunction with the Historic Houses Association.

The idea of holding the exhibition emerged when Sotheby's approached the HHA with a general offer of assistance. At that time, we were particularly concerned with the problems faced by the smaller and less well-known historic houses, which were suffering more from the general downturn in visitors than their larger, better-known counterparts. Sotheby's generously offered their rooms for an exhibition of works of art drawn from these houses, during their quiet Christmas period. The object was not only to draw attention to the houses themselves, but also to emphasize the richness and variety of their contents.

The idea was received with enthusiasm by the owners and, in all, seventy-six houses were represented by over 400 works of art, most of which had never been exhibited before. The task of selecting the objects from the huge field on offer, gathering them together and putting them on display, was a marathon by any standard. The occasion was marked by the production of a particularly fine souvenir catalogue, containing line drawings and brief historical details of all the contributing houses.

The exhibition itself brought out very clearly the difference between visiting a historic house, where the range of the furnishings reflects the changing interests and tastes of successive generations, and the more disciplined experience of visiting a museum, where objects are displayed in some form of logical order. It is the random, human element that gives historic houses their particular charm and this came across strongly. It was, indeed, a statement of what the British heritage is all about.

Over 6,000 people visited the exhibition, which received considerable press coverage, and the catalogue had to be reprinted to meet the demand. There is no doubt that the houses will benefit from the publicity. All those of us who participated are profoundly grateful to Messrs Sotheby's for their generosity and flair in mounting this most successful and original event.

A view of the exhibition in the main gallery of Sotheby's showing, in the foreground, an early nineteenth-century shell-shaped bed (Stonor Park, Henley-on-Thames, Oxfordshire) and a mechanical armillary sphere by Gault of Paris, 1741 (Dorney Court, Dorney, Windsor, Berkshire). In the background is an early Mortlake tapestry after Raphael, *circa* 1630 (Forde Abbey, Chard, Somerset). To the right of the opening is a Ming lead-glazed figure of Buddha (Haremere Hall, Etchingham, East Sussex), standing on a late eighteenth-century Swedish secretaire cabinet (Hutton-in-the-Forest, Penrith, Cumbria). Along the wall, from left to right, the three marble busts are by Joseph Nollekens, RA (Newby Hall, Ripon, Yorkshire); Joseph Wilton, RA (Capesthorne Hall, Macclesfield, Cheshire) and Roubiliac (Ripley Castle, Ripley, Harrogate, Yorkshire). Between the busts stand two George II mahogany chairs from Blair Castle, Blair Atholl, Pitlochry, Perthshire, Scotland. Standing on a Régence commode en tombeau (Manderston, Duns, Berwickshire) is an early George III musical automaton bracket clock by William Wicks (Sheldon Manor, Chippenham, Wiltshire). A Ming blue and white baluster vase (Forde Abbey) is exhibited standing on a late sixteenth or early seventeenth-century South German cabinet from Loseley House, near Guildford, Surrey. Paintings by Reynolds, PRA (Parham Park, Pulborough, West Sussex), by Batoni and Mengs (Newby Hall), and by John Wootton (Squerryes Court, Westerham, Kent) are displayed on the walls.

Notes on contributors

Shirley Bury is Keeper of Metalwork at the Victoria & Albert Museum, London. She is a specialist in silver and jewellery from the late eighteenth century to the present day and has written extensively on these subjects, contributing articles to various journals and to the catalogue of the Flaxman exhibition at the Royal Academy, London (1979). She has published a number of books, including a series on jewellery for the Victoria & Albert Museum. Her book on the *Social History of Jewellery 1795–1905* will be published next year.

T. H. Clarke joined the works of art department at Sotheby's in 1946. He specialized early in paperweights and helped to produce the first standard glossary on this subject. As a director for over twenty years, he was mainly responsible for European glass and porcelain. He is at present engaged upon cataloguing the German porcelain in the Palazzo Pitti, Florence, and completing a book on the rhinoceros in European art.

George Daniels is a consultant to Sotheby's, a past Master of the Worshipful Company of Clockmakers and a past President of the British Horological Institute. He is also a watchmaker and specializes in developing precision watches. As a horological historian, he has contributed to a number of books and he is the author of *English and American Watches* (1967), *The Art of Breguet* (1975) and *Watchmaking* (1981).

Dr Fritz Koreny is Assistant Curator of old master drawings in the Graphische Sammlung of the Albertina, Vienna. He has published *Israhel van Meckenem* (1981) and *Franz von Zülow* (1983). A catalogue of Israhel van Meckenem's engravings and a work on Albrecht Dürer's animal and plant studies are in preparation.

Souren Melikian is an art historian who has been watching the art market for many years. As an observer, he is familiar with the auction scene on both sides of the Channel, as well as the Atlantic. He founded the first weekly column covering the market as a serious news item for the *International Herald Tribune* in 1969.

Michael Moses is Associate Dean and Associate Professor of Management at the College of Business, New York University. He has just completed *Master Craftsmen of Newport: The Townsend and Goddard Families*. He has also published articles and lectured on the attribution of undocumented furniture to members of these families.

Michael O'Donoghue is Curator of the Science Reference Library at the British Museum, London, and lectures on gemmology at the City of London Polytechnic. He edits a number of journals and has published books on gemstones, minerals and man-made crystals. His most recent book, on the quartz family of gemstones, is in press.

Theodore Reff is Professor of Art History at Columbia University, New York. He organized the New York exhibition 'Degas in the Metropolitan' (1977) and, in Washington DC, the centenary exhibition 'Manet and Modern Paris' (1982–83). His publications include *The Notebooks of Edgar Degas* (1976), *Degas: The Artist's Mind* (1976), *Manet: Olympia* (1976), and a forthcoming supplement to the catalogue raisonné of Degas's paintings and pastels.

Commander Michael Saunders Watson is President of the Historic Houses Association, the representative body of all owners of historic houses, gardens and parks. He owns Rockingham Castle in Northamptonshire, which featured recently in the BBC television series *By the Sword Divided*. He is also a trustee of the Royal Botanical Gardens at Kew.

Michael Snodin is a research assistant in the Department of Prints and Drawings at the Victoria & Albert Museum, London. He is the organizer of the 1984 'Rococo' exhibition at the museum. He has published *English Silver Spoons* (1974) and *Spoons* (1976), and written articles on a variety of subjects, among them William Beckford and Regency silver.

Dr Alice Strobl is Deputy Director of the Albertina, Vienna. Among her publications are exhibition catalogues of Dürer's prints and drawings (Vienna, 1964, 1971), and the drawings of Gustav Klimt (Vienna, 1962, 1968; Essen, 1976). She has also prepared the catalogue raisonné of the drawings of Gustav Klimt, volumes I and II (1980, 1982). The third volume is due to be published at the end of 1984 and a supplementary volume is scheduled for 1985.

The following contributors are experts at Sotheby's in London: Robert Bowman, Dr Christopher de Hamel, Dr Stephen Roe and Michael R. Turner.

We would like to thank Martin Butlin, Keeper of the British Collection at the Tate Gallery, London, for contributing the note on p. 56.

PEDER SEVERIN KRØYER
The artist's wife sewing at a table
On panel, studio stamp on the reverse, 13¾in by 9¾in (35cm by 24.5cm)
London £36,300 ($50,457). 19.VI.84

Index

ENGLISH SCHOOL
A volume of watercolour designs for inn signs, eighty-four designs, mostly gouache, *circa* 1760,
page size 14in by 10in (35.5cm by 25.4cm)
London £30,800 ($42,812). 5.VII.84
From the collection of the late Lord Clark of Saltwood, OM, CH, KCB

Zin